Doing the Right Thing

Simple Solutions, Essential Tips, & Helpful
Resources for Assisting Aging Loved Ones

Doing the Right Thing

DEBBIE C. MILLER

This book was printed in the United States of America.
Order additional copies of this book from Amazon.com.

To contact the author:
Debbie@DebMiller.com
www.DebMiller.com

ISBN (paperback): 979-8-218-36349-9
ISBN (ebook): 979-8-218-44587-4

Also from the author:
Podcasts: "Move Or Improve With Debbie" (iTunes and Spotify or wherever you listen to your podcasts)
The Baby Boomer's Guide to Housing Options and How to Choose What's Right for You (Amazon)
"Multi-generational Housing: Fad or Future?" *Certified Senior Advisor (CSA) Journal* #78, Volume 1, 2020
"Relocation Anxiety" *Assisted Living Today,* June 2001

Contents

Why I Wrote This Book — 1

Selling Homes By Solving Problems — 3

Is Your Loved One a Planner or a Procrastinator? — 5

Starting the Conversation on Whether Your Loved One Should Move — 6

Eight Reasons Why Retirees Move — 7

Guidelines for Making the Best Choices — 9

What Prevents Retirees From Moving? — 11

Current Housing Choices — 12

Master Planned Communities — 13

Condominiums — 15

Advantages to Owning a Condominium — 17

Disadvantages to Owning a Condominium — 19

Active Adult Communities — 21

Questions to Ask When Considering an Active Adult Community — 23

Is It Better to Rent or Buy? — 25

Rental Apartment and Single-Family Home Communities — 28

Additional (or Accessory) Dwelling Units (ADUs) — 29

Group or Residential Care Homes — 30

Tiny Houses — 31

Multi-Generational Housing — 32

Is Multi-Generational Family Living For You? — 34

The Village Concept — 36

Modular vs. Manufactured Housing — 37

Co-Housing — 39

Live Like the Golden Girls!   40

Build or Buy New   41

Moving Abroad   45

Live in an RV!   46

Cruise the Seven Seas   48

Congregate Care or Independent Living   50

Assisted Living   51

How to Choose an Assisted Living Community That Meets Your Loved One's Needs   53

Life Plan Community or Continuing Care Retirement Community   59

Advantages of Moving to a Location Nearby   66

Downsizing/De-cluttering Tips   67

Moving Tips That Will Save You Money and Stress   69

Selling the Family Home   72

When Fixing Up to Sell the Family Home Is Not the Best Solution   76

Live or Age in Place in *Their* Home   79

Questions to Ask in Deciding Whether Your Loved One Can Age Where They Are   82

Create a Safe Space   86

Remodeling Tips for Small or Large Projects   89

Can a Reverse Mortgage Be Used to Pay for Renovations?   91

Live or Age in Place In *Your* Home   93

Can an Adult Child Refuse to Care for Their Parents?   97

Can Anyone Afford to Get Old?   98

De-clutter Whether You Move or Stay   102

Why Won't Mom Throw Anything Away?   104

How to Decide What to Keep, Sell, Donate, or Give Away   108

Guidelines to Follow in Deciding What to Do With an Item   117

What Information Should an Adult Child Obtain from Their Loved One Before They Become Incapacitated or Die?   120

End-of-Life Decisions: What You Need to Know Before They Go   128

The Importance of Planning Ahead   130

If There is a Will, There's Always a Way, Trust Me!   131

What Happens When There's No Will?   133

How Does Probate Work?   135

What Types of Property Don't Go Through Probate?   136

What's in a Trust?   137

Should Your Loved One Be Placed in Hospice Care or Receive Palliative Care?   139

How Using a Death Doula Can Help You and Your Loved One   140

Coping with Grief After Your Loss   142

"Mom Always Liked You Best"   144

What Does the Future Hold for Us?   146

Coping With Grief   147

Testimonials   149

More Stories of My Transactions as Conducted Behind the Scenes   156

Acknowledgments   165

About the Author   166

How To Reach Debbie   168

Why I Wrote This Book

I authored this book to help those responsible for the care of a parent, loved one, friend who is aging solo, or for those who want to be advocates for an older person.

As an associate broker, I have been selling real estate for over twenty-five years. As a Certified Aging in Place Specialist®, I evaluate and remodel the homes of those who want to age in place in a more accessible and safer way.

Construction and remodeling residential properties and helping seniors and adult children sell the family home are my areas of expertise. I also work with hoarders and their families to help them sort through accumulated belongings. I manage the sale of estate and trust properties (where the owner has passed away) by overseeing all the details efficiently. The systems I've developed over the years have helped me help others to achieve their goal of either selling the family home or comfortably live (or age) in place. My clients have described my services as those of "renting" a daughter (or sibling) who knows what to do, when to do it, and how to get the job done with the least amount of stress to the family.

It has taken years to develop my systems for helping others either sell the family home or age in place. I started, however, like so many of you, by necessity.

Over a period of two years in the mid-1990s, I was responsible for making decisions about the health and estates of my relatives, including my parents, in-laws, and two sets of aunts and uncles who had no children. When I started, I had little knowledge about the complexity of these types of transactions. I also realized that there were few choices and little mainstream knowledge about this field.

I quickly realized that what I learned and could share would be beneficial to Baby Boomers and others who would also walk this path. I enjoyed this aspect of real estate and decided to focus on this area as my career. It has been an amazing journey, helping many people along the way. I counsel adult children who are faced with answering the question: "What do I about mom and dad?"

The decisions an adult child must make when taking on the role of parenting their parent or loved one are varied. Unless and until you've been there, you wouldn't understand. Preparing yourself for the journey ahead is a way to ease the stress of what you'll be facing. Unfortunately, too many people wait until it's too late!

I wrote this book to help you understand the process of caring for your parent or loved one and learn as much as possible ahead of time so you can be an advocate for them. Questions you should ask and resources for helping you navigate the maze of choices are also included. In addition, by sharing stories and tips about transactions I managed, you can learn from my solutions that helped the person in need.

I dedicate this book to you, the reader, who will be an advocate for a loved one, your parents, your grandparents, or a friend who faces many decisions in achieving their care goals.

IMPORTANT NOTE: *My book contains information from my own personal experiences in the area where I do business (Virginia). Your experience may differ, depending on where you live. The questions you should ask may remain the same even though the answers may differ depending on your locality.*

Selling Homes By Solving Problems

The 2020 US Census found that the number of people older than sixty-five had grown at a rate that was five times faster than the total population increases over the previous one hundred years, and even faster in the ten years since the last US Census. By the year 2030, 72 million Americans will be sixty-five or over and the US will have, for the first time, more residents over sixty-five than children. Single women make up the largest demographic over age seventy-five. Nearly 30 percent of non-institutionalized seniors are living alone (the majority of those are women). By 2050, there will be more than 80 million seniors in the US, according to the Census Bureau.[1,2]

Retirees are making tough decisions on issues such as how long to work, when to start collecting social security, and how to survive on savings. A big decision is whether to stay in their current home or sell and move to another residence . . . or even another lifestyle . . . either close by or in another geographic location. As they age, Baby Boomers will change the face of retirement as we know it today—and builders will have to adapt to them, not the other way around. Baby Boomers are demanding novel approaches to aging, including being able to stay in their homes as long as they can. Many are opting to remodel their

1. Caplan, Zoe. "U.S. Older Population Grew from 2010 to 2020 at Fastest Rate since 1880 to 1890." Census.gov, May 25, 2023. https://www.census.gov/library/stories/2023/05/2020-census-united-states-older-population-grew.html.
2. Staff, America Counts. "2020 Census Will Help Policymakers Prepare for the Incoming Wave of Aging Boomers." Census.gov, February 25, 2022. https://www.census.gov/library/stories/2019/12/by-2030-all-baby-boomers-will-be-age-65-or-older.html.)

current home to accommodate future lifestyles since today's housing shortage is influencing their choices.

Many adult children want to help during the process but lack the information needed to help their parents or loved ones make good decisions. Many adult children are facing the realization that the roles they grew up with are being reversed and they must become parents to their parents or loved ones.

Is Your Loved One a Planner or a Procrastinator?

It's important for all parties to have complete information to make the best decisions for care—and to plan for housing needs after retirement. If seniors procrastinate, chances are good that someone else will make those decisions for them, and they may not like the outcome. Baby Boomers may have mixed emotions about leaving the family home and may wait too long to make their move. Younger Baby Boomers were born between 1955-1964, older Baby Boomers were born between 1946-1954, and there are roughly seventy million of them.

They fought in Vietnam, rocked to Elvis and the Beatles, wore miniskirts and go-go boots, and drove muscle cars with a hemi under the hood. As Baby Boomers age, their lifestyles change. They may continue to work part-time or start a new career. Fitness is an important part of the Boomer lifestyle, but they also may face unplanned health setbacks, including illness or falls. Baby Boomers will choose lifestyles that allow them to remain vibrant as long as possible, but because much of today's housing supply is not built for aging in place, Baby Boomers will lead the way in demanding solutions—and they are changing the face of retirement as we once knew it.

Starting the Conversation on Whether Your Loved One Should Move

You may begin noticing changes in your parent's or loved one's behavior. Each time you visit, each change you notice may catch you off guard. It is unexpected. What if your loved one has a major life condition and there is no plan in place? It could be a disability, a fall, onset of dementia, or any of a multitude of other possibilities. It happens every day, and, often, there is no plan. You may be called on to act on their behalf, but you do not know what to do, who to call, or who you can trust. How do you know what to plan? How to plan?

Adult children may often take part in conversations with their parents about their retirement years. Sometimes the adult child does not know what questions to ask, but they know they need to discuss the issues that may arise. The important thing to remember when starting a conversation is not to be judgmental or push them into deciding anything without investigating their options first. It may take a lot of courage on your part to start the conversation. But if you connect emotionally, ask questions, consider their perspective, and can compromise, you will go far in coming up with the best solution for your loved one. Remember, it is very likely that they are concerned about their future as well and may not know what to ask or expect. This is not a one-time conversation. The information in this book will help you navigate this difficult process.

Eight Reasons Why Retirees Move

Retirees move for many reasons, any one of which can add stress to their decision, including:

✔ They no longer need their existing space configuration. Their home is too much to maintain, or they do not need that much space (or they want more space to allow for grandchildren). The floor plan may no longer work for them (stairs are a problem or doorways and hallways that are too narrow for a wheelchair, walker, or another adult walking next to them). Why heat a five-bedroom, five-bath house for one or two people? Or rake leaves, shovel the front walk, or mow the lawn? Or pay someone to do these tasks?

✔ They want to move to a different climate (usually warmer). If they are considering buying near the water and financing the purchase, for example, the lender will require that they buy flood insurance. Obtaining flood insurance is expensive and difficult to find. Check with FEMA to learn more at www.FEMA.gov. Similarly, in these climates it is important to check for and insure against damage from sinkholes which, again, can be difficult and expensive to obtain. Refer to the Department of the Interior's map of sinkholes in the United States, which can be found at https://water.usgs.gov/edu/sinkholes/html.

✔ They want to live closer to their grandchildren. Or not, as the case may be!

✔ They prefer a different environment—urban vs. suburban vs. rural.

✔ They accept a job in a different area.

✔ They move due to health reasons. They may not have a choice if they become unable to function on their own through mental illness, sensory impairment, or being unable to perform activities of daily living (ADLs) including personal hygiene or grooming, getting dressed, using the toilet, eating, and moving around on their own. Instrumental activities of daily living consist of things your parents do every day to take care of themselves and the home they live in. These tasks include using the telephone, shopping, preparing meals, housekeeping, using transportation, taking medication(s), and managing finances.

✔ They want to reduce their taxes and lower their cost of living. Keep in mind that states with no income tax will often have higher real estate taxes or other forms of taxation to make up the difference. There are websites showing lists of the States and their tax structure, including taxfoundation.org.

✔ They also want access to good medical facilities, convenient transportation, and recreational and social amenities. It's important to help them make choices that will accommodate them as they age. They may be in good health today, but what about ten years from now? It will be much harder to pack up and move when they are older. **And too many wait until it's too late!**

Guidelines for Making the Best Choices

It's important to check taxes (real estate and income), year-round weather, cost of living, crime rate, the quality of health care, and cultural and social opportunities in the new location. Plan to visit for at least a long weekend, preferably longer. Visit when the weather is the worst. Florida in January is different from Florida in July! Arizona with 120-degree temperatures in summer may convince them to consider living in the state all year but split their time between southern Arizona in winter and northern Arizona in summer. Homeowner insurance costs are also rising and often needed, even if they pay cash for their home.

Many retirees would consider moving if the process did not seem so overwhelming. It's a big task to find the perfect place. The Baby Boomer generation prefers communities with a variety of recreational choices. Bocce ball and pickleball courts are replacing tennis courts (tennis exerts too much pressure on elbows, arms, and ankles); golf is no longer a "must have" requirement (courses are getting too costly to maintain and Boomers don't play as much golf as their parents). And there are communities that built golf courses as an amenity but were converted to something else. What Baby Boomers want will affect a builder's development of a community and changes over time. They will include small movie theaters, or communities for like-minded retirees, such as musicians or artists, nudists, even pilots. Baby Boomers are a large group that builders want to please.

There are communities that were built years ago to accommodate an older generation. These communities can be explored to see if the budget meets their environment. It may be better to spend more to get more. Make a list of priorities and have your loved one compare notes with their spouse or partner if they have one. Divide the list into "must have," "would like to have," and "not important." Retirees want convenient access to social activities outside the community as well as in the community. High-quality medical facilities nearby are important. Communities that are close to a college often provide access to teaching facilities for lifelong learning educational experiences and social interaction. Courses are available online, so if they love a different location not close to a college and don't need social interaction, they can access the classes on their computer. But the in-person interaction provides stimulating conversation that they wouldn't necessarily get online.

How convenient is the community to shopping, restaurants, public transportation, airports, etc.? Doctors and hospital facilities should be found so they can get to them in an emergency or when needed for regular visits.

What are the taxes they will pay in the state(s) they are considering? Will the property they are interested in need eventual upgrades? Be sure to budget for general maintenance issues such as eventual roof replacement, furnace/air conditioner, etc.

NOTES:

What Prevents Retirees From Moving?

Often, parents don't have the energy or resources to make a move. They may be resistant to change or unsure of what lifestyle is best for them. Their adult children may or may not be able to help them in their decision. Stubbornness in staying where they are helps them protect their sense of independence. Reading this book can help both groups to move forward with the best solution. Too many times, I have seen what happens to older adults who waited too long to decide. A fall, stroke, or other health emergency changes their choices and future. I've talked with clients who do not want a particular apartment in a community when it's offered to them. I tell them to "move in to move up." Moving in gets them on the "insiders" wait-list where they'll be able to choose another apartment sooner than someone who is still on the outside waiting list. Now is a good time to sell the family home. There is a scarcity of available housing right now so selling sooner rather than later is something to consider. Imagine all the inventory that will be on the market when all the other age-in-place Boomers decide to sell! Housing values will drop too. Even though there's not a lot of choice in active adult housing, buying something new is a great feeling when compared to the money spent fixing up an existing home to live in for a while longer.

Current Housing Choices

Your loved ones may be evaluating their housing options as they age. Many want to age (or live) in place. But others are looking at other options as they decide which choice works best for them. Weighing their options includes knowing the terms and definitions for the types of housing currently available. Use the options covered here to learn about options they may want to explore. **The biggest mistake people make is waiting too long to decide.**

NOTES:

Master Planned Communities

These communities are popular choices for retirees. These are large neighborhoods, built on previously undeveloped acreage, with many recreational and entertainment amenities for the residents. These communities provide social outreach and a nostalgic sense of neighborly interaction. There may be weekly local farmers' markets, and biking, golfing, jogging will physically connect the small-town residents with each other. Medical facilities are often close by as well. They do have housing for all ages and there may also be a section reserved for those over the age of fifty-five.

The variety of amenities allows neighbors to bond over common interests, whether well-loved or newly found. From sharing a glass of wine with friends, or attending art exhibits or other locally tailored topics, there will be a myriad of choices. These communities are usually inter-generational in concept. It's not unusual for families to move here. The seniors may have their own section of the community with their own activities. There are also builders who build a wing off the main living space for the grandparents while the family has their own space under the same roof. This helps both parties since the grandparents are now close by to provide childcare or interact with their grandchildren easily and the parents are close by in case the grandparents need attention.

A monthly fee is charged to live here. The fee depends on how many amenities are offered, how large the community is, as well as landscaping and maintenance of the common grounds. Think twice before buying in a golf course community. The greens require a lot of water and maintenance to maintain. It's better to buy in a community that does not have a golf course within its boundaries. Look for one that has courses outside the community and is convenient to get to. Let someone else maintain that pretty look! I have known people who bought in a golf-course community only to discover that the golf course was sold to an outside company who re-developed it into a playing field with bright lights on at night.

The homeowners association (HOA) is the governing body that handles managing and maintaining the shared areas and shared elements. They enforce the rules, which may include noise levels, pet policies, guest visitation, parking, and more. Many people do not want a planned community as everything looks the same, but it's the consistency that keeps the value up.

NOTES:

Condominiums

Active adults may choose to live in urban areas where they can walk to shopping, restaurants, and nightlife. Empty nesters should realize that they may be bidding for a condominium against first-time buyers. Baby Boomers can often outbid younger buyers because they offer cash for the property. Moving from a single-family home into a condominium requires an understanding of the difference between living in a building where a board of directors makes the rules vs. a community where rules may be non-existent or less stringent. Condominium living gives the owner freedom to "lock and leave" if they travel extensively. The owner handles maintaining everything inside the unit walls. The condominium association maintains everything outside those walls. Carefully read all information in the re-sale or condominium association documents and the reserve study. The association hires an outside consultant to develop a complete analysis of the community and the costs to make improvements such as elevator repair/replacement, parking lot paving, redecorating the lobby, roof replacement, and more. A portion of the monthly fee is set aside in a reserve fund to pay for repairs or improvements to the building(s). Condominium fees will rise to cover the costs of maintaining the exterior and interior shared, or common, areas of the building. There may be special assessments on older buildings to cover big expenses like window replacement, elevators, balcony railings, or parking lot re-surfacing. Read the rules and bylaws for any condominium building under consideration, and state law usually allows the potential buyer the right to void the transaction if they do not like what they find in the documents. For example, are pets allowed? If so, is there a size limitation? Are there special assessments coming up and will the current owner pay for those costs? Is it possible to rent a unit and if so, for how long? Many associations allow for only a certain number of units to be rented out and often the owner must have lived in the unit for a minimum period of two years. Be sure to find out before you buy! Educate yourself and read ALL the documents carefully. Review the pros and cons below.

NOTES:

Advantages to Owning a Condominium

- A condominium is often less expensive to buy than a single-family home. Many Baby Boomers use the cash they receive from the sale of their house to pay cash for their condominium. Others prefer financing to take advantage of interest deductions on their tax returns. If the condominium will be owned for at least five years, it may be a wise investment.

- The shared areas, landscaping, elevators, hallways, lobbies, and building exterior are owned, managed, and kept by the condominium association, or HOA (homeowners association). If there is a clubhouse, the HOA will maintain the amenities, too. The owner pays a monthly fee, as do the other owners, to pay someone else to complete these tasks. These fees will increase over time. If the purchase is financed, the lender will factor the monthly fees in determining the monthly mortgage amount the buyer can afford. The more amenities the condominium has, the higher the monthly fees. Units higher up in the building often have a higher price tag. Especially if it is a water view that is amazing!

- The unit owners can "lock and leave" since the owner doesn't have to worry about maintenance. Plan for mail delivery while away for a length of time. The local post office can hold your mail.

- Many people don't want to buy in a planned community. Everything looks the same, but consistency keeps the value up.

- Is there a security system of some kind, on-site management, an elevator or two, a pool (indoor and/or outdoor depending on the weather), fitness center, bocce ball and/or tennis, gardening areas, and more?

✔ Choose the condominium based on location, amenities, age of the building, and whether the value has increased over time.

✔ Is parking available? Is it an unreserved space, reserved open space, garage, or other provision? If the space is bought separately, is it recorded on the Deed so it can be sold later? If it's not needed, can it be included as a benefit if it is sold with the property?

NOTES:

Disadvantages to Owning a Condominium

✔ Condominium fees and special assessments aren't under the owner's individual control, so be sure to ask what assessments have been levied in the past and what assessments are planned. Owners will also pay real estate taxes and insurance, and long-term maintenance of appliances, HVAC, etc.

✔ Living in a community requires everyone to be more respectful of the needs and rights of other residents.

✔ If the market shifts downward, owners may "walk away" from their mortgages and monthly fee payment. If owners aren't paying their monthly fees, then there won't be enough funds to support the community.

✔ When reviewing the condominium documents, look for the parking restrictions, ability to rent, maintenance, and more. If it is in a fifty-five-plus community, there will be restrictions as to how long guests (including children and grandchildren) can visit.

✔ In certain instances, failure to pay the monthly fee can result in the board taking legal action. Be sure to read the condominium documents before completing the purchase transaction. The documents will explain what the covenants, conditions, and restrictions are by which owners must abide. Read over the minutes of recent board meetings and review the financial records to make sure the association is solvent, and no pending lawsuits are in the works.

✔ If the association hasn't planned, there can be a shortfall in the budget for big-ticket items such as paving the parking lot, repairing roads, elevator repair (or replacement), replacing roofs, and more. A special assessment will be levied to cover these exterior maintenance costs.

✔ When visiting an established community, talk to residents to find out what it's like to live there. Is the community well-kept? Are residents mostly satisfied with how things are run daily? Have there been any lawsuits recently or expected at a future point? How well are insurance claims managed? Is the association management company reputable and competent?

✔ **IMPORTANT**: If buying in an elevator building, remember that, in case of fire or emergency evacuation, the elevators are **NOT** accessible. This means walking down flights of stairs to evacuate. And if there's a fire, there must be a backup plan for removing or saving important files! Waking up in the middle of the night from a deep sleep, time is of the essence to evacuate so know what to grab. Purchase a fire-proof safe to hold important papers. If not, at least decide where to store those papers off-site or upload documents onto a thumb drive to take away. An evacuation plan is important in emergency situations.

NOTES:

Active Adult Communities

These are gated communities for the fifty-five-plus age group, with a centralized area for activities such as swimming, tennis, bocce ball, track, fitness centers, etc. They often include walking and biking trails. They don't provide health-related services but may be part of a larger community of continuing care if health problems develop. These communities should be near a hospital and medical facilities. These communities are considered "aging at home" so they don't offer assisted living or health care facilities. If your parent(s) need medical care, they will have to contract with their own homecare provider.

Communities have single-family and villa-style homes that are low-maintenance. Additionally, communities may have condominiums. Smaller communities may be condominiums or townhomes only. A monthly fee takes care of the maintenance of the grounds and community center and, often, lawn care as well. Visitors' stays are often restricted to a certain time limit (perhaps two weeks at a time, which allows for grandchildren to visit). List the activities most attractive to your loved one and check with the activities director to see the schedule of events. There should be a variety of things to do, and access to them should be included in the monthly fee. Talk to the residents, tour the community, and visit for at least a weekend, not only to explore the community but also the surrounding area. Visit grocery stores to check prices, find the closest hospital and more. There are communities where activities, such as golf, can be accessed through a separate membership.

Because of the age requirement, it becomes harder to sell the home to a willing younger buyer. It will be interesting, when the active adults move on due to moving into assisted living or death, to see whether younger buyers will want the same surroundings for their retirement. There's a commonality among communities regarding amenities, housing choices, and other "McDonald-like" features. Regardless of where you are in the US, a McDonald's Big Mac is the same. Active adult communities tend to have homes that look similar but have a choice of exterior looks and are limited to a range of builder-provided choices inside and outside. The location of the home within the community is important and the location of the community within the local area may be the deciding factor in their decision on which to buy. Buying a home near the pool or bocce ball court may be noisier, even if it is more convenient to the centrally found amenities of the community.

Many active adult communities have a higher percentage of couples living there. If you are aging solo, you may prefer a different choice.

NOTES:

Questions to Ask When Considering
an Active Adult Community

✔ Since the community is age-restricted, will your parents be content living only among people their age? There are restrictions as to how long guests can stay. Seeing the grandchildren on a regular basis may prevent longer visits, so consider this restriction carefully. If family isn't close by, then this restriction may help in making new friends.

✔ What other restrictions are there? Read the homeowner association's (HOA) rules during the negotiations. Are there restrictions on changing the color of the exterior of your home? Can different exterior paint colors be used? The rules will tell you if this is restricted to certain colors. What happens to the house when it's no longer occupied? Discuss this with an estate planning attorney to make the right decision. Also ask whether the property can be rented, and for how long. Consider renting instead of buying in a community, if that's a possibility. Find out about restrictions regarding renting vs. buying. In many instances, failure to pay the monthly fees can result in legal action against the owner by the association.

✔ What costs are included or not included in the monthly fee? The fee should include maintenance of the shared areas and other specifics. At some point, as a community ages, there will be a "special assessment" on the entire community to maintain the amenities. Costly renovations aren't unusual in older communities. Check the budgets for the past several years to see what special assessments have been levied and talk to owners to find out if any large-scale projects are planned. These fees may take a large chunk of savings since they are outside the monthly costs of living in the community.

✔ What activities are available? Do residents have input introducing new ones? If you play golf but don't want to pay for one that's part of the community, find out how many golf courses are close by outside the community. It may be less expensive to golf elsewhere rather than pay hefty fees to maintain a golf course in the community. Participating in new activities is an effective way to make new friends.

NOTES:

Is It Better to Rent or Buy?

This decision is a major consideration in planning for retirement since the financial aspect will affect your loved one's life and budget for years.

Advantages of Owning

- ✔ Buying a home provides security that's not available with renting. Control of daily living is something not achieved by renting. A fixed-rate mortgage benefits owners since they know that the monthly cost will not increase. Taxes, HOA fees, and utility costs will increase but the loan remains constant.

- ✔ The property value will increase over time, especially if ownership is over several years. The owner builds equity since the monthly mortgage payments are paying down the principal balance. Equity provides the possibility to borrow against it to finance improvements using a home equity loan or line of credit (HELOC) or pay for unanticipated medical expenses.

- ✔ Because the owner owns the home, they can decorate the way they like. Keep in mind that in a homeowner association (HOA), the owner may be limited as to what they can landscape outside. But the interior is all theirs so it's okay to change the paint color, replace the tile, add lighting—the list is endless!

- ✔ Depending on the location, buying may be more advantageous than renting. It depends on interest rates, location, and amenities.

- ✔ How will the purchase be financed? There are options available for seniors, but they require careful consideration. Reverse mortgages, FHA loans, conventional loans, VA loans, HECM for Purchase loans, and more. ALL require careful consideration. Read the fine print. Often seniors sell their current home and pay cash for their next home.

✔ AARP surveyed seniors and found that 94 percent of borrowers felt that a reverse mortgage gave them peace of mind (AARP Public Policy Institute, December 2007). Eighty-nine percent indicated that their lifestyle is more comfortable and 87 percent felt that their reverse mortgage improved their quality of life. The main advantage of a reverse mortgage is that the traditional mortgage payment is eliminated. It can be an effective way to age in place and the funds can be used to provide at-home care. The home cannot be taken from the owner due to non-payment of a traditional mortgage. It's best to own the home free and clear of any current mortgage, or the existing balance is low enough to be paid off using the reverse mortgage. There are other restrictions, and owners must get counseling before the loan is issued. The money received is tax-free too and neither the owner nor the estate will ever owe more than the home's value when the loan is paid off. The FHA (Federal Housing Administration) insures the loan. Although there are no monthly mortgage payments, the owner must pay insurance and real estate taxes and maintain the property. Owners must use the residence for a minimum of 6 months a year. The improvements to reverse mortgages make this option one to consider carefully and seriously. It's not the reverse mortgage of old.

Advantages of Renting

In real estate, it's said that people who rent are contributing to the landlord's retirement, not theirs. The tenant doesn't own the property; thus, they aren't building equity. But sometimes it makes sense to rent.

Renters need a place to live, and it may be that buying doesn't make sense for their situation.

- ✔ When buying, a down payment and closing costs related to the purchase are needed. Renting requires a security deposit and, if a pet is going to occupy the property and the landlord will accept Rover or Fifi, they'll ask for a pet deposit to cover the cost of any damage the pet may cause while the tenant lives there.

- ✔ Renting makes sense if your loved one is still deciding where to live and needs time to evaluate locations. The lease covers a specified time which allows the tenant time to explore long-term options.

- ✔ Property taxes or maintenance of the home are the landlord's responsibility. If something breaks (water heater starts to leak, air conditioning isn't working on a ninety-degree day, roof leaks, or other) it's the landlord's responsibility to fix it. Hopefully, it won't take too long to get the problem resolved. It's tough to go without air conditioning in intense heat for too long. And if there's a water leak, be sure that no mold has appeared as a result.

NOTES:

Rental Apartment and
Single-Family Home Communities

There are senior communities that are either being built or retrofitted to accommodate seniors looking for luxury. These properties include a variety of restaurants, on-site nursing, chauffeurs, beauty and barber salons, lifelong learning, and more. These units have a luxury price tag, too. But for those seniors with the money to support the lifestyle, this choice is often a welcome change since they can live in a terrific location and have amenities galore. Especially appealing is the convenience of moving quickly and easily.

There are also low-cost rentals which, for those on a fixed budget, may be ideal. A senior can rent from month-to-month or yearly. There are activities on-site, and parking is provided. There are also areas for eating communally. This may be a good choice if your loved ones are unsure of the area and want to "try it on" for a while before making a final decision. These buildings were constructed with the intent of housing retirees and providing amenities for residents on a short-term basis. In today's market, builders recognize that a build-to-rent option is popular with Baby Boomers. They don't want a mortgage and renting gives them flexibility to move without the hassle of selling.

Builders are recognizing the appeal of a single-family rental home for seniors who don't want a neighbor above them. They can still enjoy a managed community with crews to take care of the shared areas and they know that they can move easily when the lease is up. These communities are a welcome alternative for those who want the freedom to move and don't need or want the mortgage interest deduction.

Additional (or Accessory) Dwelling Units (ADUs)

Designed for one or two people, an additional or accessory dwelling unit (ADU), also called a granny flat or granny pod, is a self-contained living space often located on the lot of a single-family home. It can also be in-house or an addition to the existing home. It's a convenient way for families to accommodate aging parents. As multigenerational housing becomes more accepted and needed, granny pods are likely to become more prevalent if districts revise zoning laws to accommodate extended families. Zoning laws often determine if this approach is a good one. Several counties already provide special approval for elderly housing on a single-family site, but more communities need to change the zoning laws to allow for this solution. The pods are self-contained and can include video cameras to allow caregivers to check in remotely. The flooring is softer, to minimize injury if the resident falls. There are safety rails and other special accommodations. The price will be a factor for many. Although a granny pod can pay for itself in a few years, the base price plus installation can be well over $100,000-$200,000, depending on the area of the country and the amenities. The budget should also allow for extra in-home care. Several states have approved this living arrangement if the resident's doctor has ordered it.

Group or Residential Care Homes

This living arrangement provides a higher level of care than assisted living. It's more personalized care since there are fewer residents. Typically, a residential care home provides a single or double room (not an apartment). Residents share a bathroom, meals, housekeeping. Personal care is available too. Most homes provide supervision and have staff to help with activities of daily living (bathing, dressing, toileting, etc.) Medical-level care like tube feeding, for example, is not provided. They do accept private payment, money from VA Aid & Attendance, and long-term care insurance. If your loved one doesn't feel comfortable in an institutional kind of living situation, this choice may be acceptable to them. They can still go shopping, have friends and family visit, eat out, and more. Each state has its own directory of licensed residential care homes so you can verify that they're properly licensed.

NOTES:

Tiny Houses

The tiny house concept has been around for several years. In various areas of the country, they may be known as accessory or additional dwelling Units (ADUs). Older adults can use them for second homes since they're less expensive to build, heat, maintain, and repair. Taxes are also lower. Living with a smaller footprint requires a simpler lifestyle that is less cluttered. Tiny houses are usually fewer than -500 square feet and rarely exceed 1,000 square feet. Zoning laws and building code size restrictions can influence the size. Agility is needed to access the sleeping area, which is often in a loft area accessible by ladder or stairs. A tiny house can be a welcome "second home" on an existing residential home's lot. Watch for tiny houses to be built in clusters so that chores can be shared and a small community of people with similar needs can be created.

NOTES:

Multi-Generational Housing

A recent report by RentCafe (November 2023) indicated that 20 percent of millennials and 68 percent of Generation Z still live with other family members. About a third of those say they plan to stay there for at least two to five years. Younger generations find it more appealing to live in their parent's home to save money on expenses and save for a down payment on a home of their own. This allows families with inter-generational relatives to live under one roof. Everyone will need his or her own space, privacy, and separate entrance. This solution is becoming more popular as the population ages. Having an aging parent or loved one under the same roof as the adult child eases the stress of knowing that their loved ones are safe, and they can be helped quickly in case of an accident or another emergency. Homebuilders have recognized this need and are filling it by designing houses in communities that can accommodate generational needs. For existing houses, an addition can provide an in-law apartment with its own entrance, depending on local building restrictions. If this route is chosen, be sure to have a written contract between the parties living there so boundaries are set up ahead of time. What does multi-generation housing look like? There can be duplexes (two houses side-by-side) sharing one wall or an upper and lower configuration. In certain areas, triplexes or fourplexes are available. These are great to own. You live in one, and your parents or loved one live in the other. If you own a triplex or fourplex, renting the other ones out brings in rent to cover the mortgage cost plus provide extra money to cover expenses. There are casitas in Hawaii which are apartments attached to the main home. Casitas are also found in

Rhode Island, California, Arizona, Nevada, Texas, and other warm cities. The predominant locations for multi-family housing are Arizona, Nevada, California, Texas, and Washington state. I've remodeled split foyer homes that have outside access in the lower level through a sliding glass door. The lower level is converted to an in-law suite. Current zoning laws in many districts are antiquated and need revision for multi-generational living to be widely used.

NOTES:

Is Multi-Generational Family Living For You?

To decide if multi-generational housing is something you want to pursue, discuss these issues:

- ✔ Is your home compatible for everyone involved? Are there too many stairs that would prevent a loved one from being with other family members? Does a bathroom need renovating to accommodate an older adult?

- ✔ Hold family meetings to discuss issues. This will be helpful in avoiding or solving problems. Decide how much, if any, child-care you want your parents to provide? Are there tasks that a grandchild could perform to help their grandparents? Realize that as children get older, they may not want to spend time with their grandparents. They have more freedom to spend time with friends and be involved in outside activities.

- ✔ Ensure that everyone has their own space. A large bedroom addition with an ensuite bathroom is a plus for grandparents. Devoted areas for grandchildren to play or do homework should be set aside as well. What sound level (TV or music) is too loud?

- ✔ Do your housekeeping standards match each other? How often do you vacuum, what days do you do laundry, mow the lawn, or do other household chores? Co-existing is much easier if everyone handles doing what they can to help around the house and care for the older adults.

✔ Dispose of extra furniture that prevents safety. Declutter to avoid falls. Consider re-arranging the furniture to provide a better path throughout the house.

✔ Most importantly, be sure that your house can accommodate multi-generational living. Tight bathrooms, too many levels, narrow hallways, and poor lighting are features that may need adjusting or upgrading. Budget accordingly.

✔ Is your immediate family overly protective of their possessions? Family members need to like each other and share interests. Habits should be compatible and all should be willing to create harmony in the household.

This living arrangement can help ease childcare which saves money for the parents if the grandparents are willing to help. Parents should not expect grandparents to be on call twenty-four seven, though. This living arrangement can also help when an older family member has health issues. Adult children can help and supervise their care and teenagers can socialize with them. Be aware that, unlike childcare which often gets easier as the child grows, elder care can get more difficult over time, especially if the grandparent has dementia or mobility issues. The cost savings of keeping grandparents close by is a plus, but it will increase the stress level of the primary care provider.

NOTES:

The Village Concept

The Village Movement is a nationwide network of non-profit membership organizations. Each village helps local seniors live independently in their homes. Nearly fifty of these non-profit organizations currently exist in the country. Operated by board members or volunteers who design and administer daily operations, members pay annual dues, depending on the village structure. When a member needs aid beyond the capabilities of volunteers or neighbors, the village offers a concierge service for local businesses prescreened for security. Volunteers and/or neighbors provide personal, wellness, technological transportation, and household services along with home repairs. Tasks range from changing light bulbs, installing a DVD player, uploading programs in a computer, or housekeeping chores such as helping with laundry, gardening, dog walking, grocery shopping, changing sheets on a mattress, and transportation to medical appointments. This concept is based on an "aging in place" belief that people want to remain in their homes as long as possible.

NOTES:

Modular vs. Manufactured Housing

The US is suffering from a severe housing affordability crisis. Much of it is due to a supply shortage that can't be solved quickly with today's construction methods along with a lack of skilled construction labor. Modular building is a promising method to increase the supply of affordable housing. It's an option that should be considered.

Modular constructed homes are factory-built modules which are then shipped to a home site where the sections are assembled. The homes are well-built, and owners can obtain financing through traditional lenders. Custom modular-built homes are growing in popularity since rising labor costs, increasing regulations, and other factors are making this possibility a practical choice. They are overbuilt (from a building code perspective) because they must survive the transport and placement by crane on the home's foundation.

Do NOT confuse a modular home with a manufactured home which conforms to the National Manufactured Home Construction and Safety Standards Act of 1976 and is enforced by the Department of Housing and Urban Development. Previously known as mobile homes, HUD now regulates the home's design and construction, strength and durability, fire resistance, energy efficiency and quality control. Tough performance standards are in place which regulate heating, plumbing, air-conditioning, and thermal and electrical systems.

Manufactured homes are popular in rural areas on private land with minimal land-use restrictions. They can also be placed in a land-lease community. Mobile homes are an affordable choice if budgets are limited. They are placed on a block foundation to save costs. Look for a label verifying that the home was built to the HUD building code. It's usually under the sink or near the electric panel box. There will also be a metal label on the exterior of each section. The labels will tell you the state code for which the home conforms.

Modular homes, however, are based on the same codes as site-built homes. The various building codes of a given authority are what govern the construction. The modular home is transported on a carrier. The home is taken off the carrier and transferred onto a foundation. This type of home can be customized and built to exact tolerances and is energy efficient.

NOTES:

Co-Housing

This form of housing community can appeal to all ages. People (who may or may not know each other) live in their own homes but have shared areas outside the home. People are there for each other when and as needed. A central board of residents oversees the decision-making and budget, with input from residents. Owners pay their own real estate taxes and contribute a monthly fee toward the cost of amenities. There are communities that center around the "tiny house" concept which lowers the monthly costs and maintenance.

NOTES:

Live Like the Golden Girls!

Remember Blanche (Rue McClanahan), Sophia (Estelle Getty), Rose (Betty White), and Dorothy (Bea Arthur)? The popular eighties sitcom involving four previously married women living together in Miami? They became roommates after living a full life and raising their children. Retirement meant taking risks to find new purpose in their lives. They lived under one roof and shared expenses. This is a choice if each person can adapt to living under one roof with others and not overstep their boundaries. It's possible to hire a person to do odd jobs and help as needed too. In a college town, having students available to do these jobs can help the residents enjoy their life more and provide some income for the students!

NOTES:

Build or Buy New

When considering the purchase of a new home from a builder, consider these factors:

- ✔ Using a Realtor® experienced in new home construction will help a great deal. A builder may tell a potential buyer that they can get a better deal if they don't use a Realtor® but understand that the builder's representative is representing the builder—not the buyer. If a potential buyer currently owns their home and is moving into a new place, the Realtor® can negotiate the move-in date with the builder and coordinate the sale of the buyer's current home to meet those contract deadlines. The Realtor® also knows the local builders and how to work with them. A local Realtor® can refer someone to a Realtor® in their new location if moving a long distance. The Realtor® can also assist the buyers with finish choices.

- ✔ Be sure to have a thorough home inspection. Buyers may think that this isn't necessary since the home is new. Ideally, the home inspection should cover three phases of construction. First, inspect the foundation. Second, inspect the framing and electrical/plumbing prior to drywall installation. Third, inspect after the drywall is hung and the house is close to completion. The inspector will provide a "punch list" of items to be corrected by the builder before the owner takes possession. Builders offer a one-year warranty (starting after settlement) which allows the owner to find defects and create a reference list of issues so those items can be fixed as well. These fixes are completed before the builder's warranty expires.

✔ The builder provides a limited number of finishes (cabinets, flooring, trim, appliances, and more). It can be overwhelming to make that many decisions within an abbreviated time limit! It's okay to not use the builder's tile or lights, etc. Just get it in writing.

✔ Research the builder's reputation as well as that of the community and surrounding area first—talk to neighbors, visit the community for a weekend, check the distance to health-care facilities, grocery stores, shopping, and restaurants, and more. Checking prices will help your loved one decide if they can afford the area as well as the residence they want to buy.

✔ Consider resale value: choose square footage and location in the community over upgrades. Appliances can be upgraded later, but the location of the home will remain the same. Don't "over-improve" more than the neighbors. Too much personal customization will make it harder to sell later.

✔ Walk the floor plan. Even if the builder offers virtual reality technology, walking inside the house with the chosen floor plan is important. It's an effective way to visualize where furniture will go. Remember that model homes are staged with new furniture to show lifestyle. Look beyond the furniture and wall hangings. Imagine how the furniture and art, etc. that YOU own will fit in the space.

✔ Have an attorney experienced in builder contracts review the documents and explain them. Builders prefer to use their own contracts.

✔ Builders will often have a preferred lender and a preferred settlement company. They'll encourage the buyer to use their companies since it streamlines the process for them. But buying a home is a big expense so don't be afraid to ask for quotes from other trusted lenders and settlement companies before signing with those preferred by the builder. Use the other quotes to negotiate a better deal such as a lower interest rate or upgrades with the builder.

Since your loved one will be aging (living) in place in their new home, include, at least, these features:

✔ **Entry:** Preferably a no-step entrance into a wide foyer. The entry should have a roof over it to keep it dry. If they enter the home from a garage, the entrance from the garage to the interior should also provide easy access. Inside, be sure there's enough open space in which to move around while they enter and leave.

✔ **Lighting:** Check after dark to be sure there's adequate outside lighting. This theme should continue to the interior. Install large, easy-to-read house numbers in a prominent place outside so they can be read easily day or night. A fire and rescue team needs to find the home quickly in an emergency.

✔ **Flooring:** Should be non-slip and easy to walk on. Choices include cork, linoleum, wood, and even rubber flooring. If carpet is chosen, select a low-pile carpet that's easy to walk on or roll over (by a wheelchair or walker). Use scatter rugs judiciously, if at all, since falls are common for older adults.

✔ **Floor Plan:** Many new homes include all the required minimum features, such as a full bath, kitchen, and a master bedroom on the main level. Often, builders include a floor plan with an upper level to accommodate guests and grandchildren. Doorways should be thirty-six inches wide and hallways should be forty-two inches wide. Handrails should be mounted on at least one side of any stairs. Windows should be easy to open. Thermostats should be easy to reach and be no more than forty-four to forty-eight inches above the floor. Rocker panel light switches should be thirty-six to forty-four inches above the floor and electrical outlets should be eighteen to twenty-four inches above the floor.

✔ **Bathroom:** The master bathroom needs plenty of floor space to accommodate a wheelchair or care provider. A walk-in or roll-in shower with non-slip flooring should also include a built-in shower bench. Lever handles should be used on the sink faucets and shower. An adjustable hand-held shower faucet is ideal. Toilets that sit seventeen to nineteen inches off the floor make them easier to use. Kohler and Toto are good examples of toilets that are easy to use. And they have warm seats and washlet features.

✔ **Kitchen:** Pull-out and adjustable shelving makes meal preparation easier. Countertops should have rounded edges and an area with open space underneath so that food can be prepared while the resident is seated. Side-by-side or drawer-style refrigerators are helpful as well. Instead of a higher breakfast bar, opt for table-height seating for eating.

✔ **Laundry:** Front-loading washers and dryers that are elevated twelve to fifteen inches off the floor will make it easier to reach the clothes. If the floorplan allows it, locate the laundry area on the main level near the master bedroom rather than in the basement or garage.

✔ Allow for the possibility of adding an elevator later if there is an upper level. Although expensive to install, an elevator provides access to all the space in the home.

Moving Abroad

As housing expenses rise and affordability becomes an issue, coupled with the lack of ample housing in the US, many retirees move to countries that welcome expats to their shores. An excellent resource to help decide what country may be best and answer questions about what a country's requirements are, can be found on International Living's website (www.internationalliving.com). They have information to start the search and help in deciding which location works best. I've interviewed several expats on my podcast to see what they like and don't like about international living. One point to mention is that of health care. Be sure to check on the quality and availability of health care in a foreign country before moving there.

NOTES:

Live in an RV!

Recreational vehicles (RV) are a popular retirement choice among couples and solo agers as well. I've worked with several clients over the years who simply sold the house and their possessions and lived a carefree retirement in an RV. They first thought they would travel for a few months, then the adventure turned into a year. They kept on going for another year. This may be the perfect solution for your loved one. They shouldn't be surprised to find waiting lists to rent an RV (they should try before they buy). There are websites (www.Rvesy.com) which are like an Airbnb but for recreational vehicles. The sites feature RVs throughout the US, including towable, motor homes, pet-friendly RVs, and more. If both parents are driving it, be sure they both feel comfortable handling the operation of whichever one they choose. They'll either fall in love with this way of living, or they will decide it is not for them. Slightly more than 10 million US households own RVs and about one million Americans live in theirs full time. Choose the rig that's easiest to drive. When a car is towed behind a motorhome, it's known as a "toad." Sticks and bricks refer to a permanent home. Class A are big vehicles. Class B are vans, and Class C have a truck cab attached to an RV chassis. Fifth wheels are the big RVs pulled by trucks. Class A has large living areas with many amenities, often with a slide-out to increase the interior space. It's an excellent choice for longer trips. However, they're expensive to buy, repair, insure, and fill up the tank. Check ahead with the states that will be visited to find which ones require a special license to drive Class A. Class B are less expensive to buy, fuel, and repair. They're an excellent choice for a solo traveler or a weekend away. They're referred to as car vans or van campers. They have a raised roof to allow for more headroom when standing or walking. Class B vans are the easiest to drive. Class C combines the best of Class A and Class B. It's versatile, drivable, and more affordable. Class C is built on a truck chassis and can be twenty-two to thirty-three feet long and has an extra cab jutting out over the driver's compartment that holds a bed. There's an area that converts to a bed, kitchen, and bathroom. When taking driving lessons, opt for the Class A lessons. They're offered through RVDriving school. RVersity on YouTube also teaches driving. RV Education 101 is another source. Video courses are available too. It's a good idea to rent for a weekend to practice maneuvering. If two or more adults are traveling together, be sure all drivers can handle the RV. For more information on full-time traveling, check out Wand'erly Magazine. Learn about RV insurance, maintenance costs, roadside assistance (there is a company called CoachNet that is the equivalent of AAA for RVs), cost of a campsite, cost of fuel, and more. Know how to handle mail while away and go paperless as much as possible. Automatic bill pay can handle regular bills. There's a company called Traveling Mailbox that can scan mail and forward it to any address, and deposit checks. Mail can be checked from anywhere in the world if a good internet connection is available. At some point, putting down some roots may sound like a promising idea. There are RV communities with like-minded explorers. There's a physical neighborhood but there's also freedom to travel when wanted. There are websites that list communities that offer this type of living (www.BestPlacesToRetire.com and www.seniormobile.com are two of many).

Cruise the Seven Seas

There are retirees who decide to sell (or rent) their home and most of their belongings and travel the world while they can still live independently. Cruise ships include food and a cabin to sleep in, housekeeping, enrichment activities, and the ability to travel the world without boarding planes, booking hotels, or packing and unpacking! The cost to live aboard a ship depends on the type of cabin chosen, laundry, how often the guests fly "home" to visit family, gratuities for the ship's staff, land excursions offered by the ship, and how often a passenger wants to dine in one the of the upscale dining rooms instead of the basic buffet. Alcohol is usually extra, depending on the type of drink package chosen. Several cruise ships offer the opportunity to buy or lease a cabin. Advantages include no grocery shopping, no deciding what is for dinner tonight, and no home maintenance hassles. Voyages can be booked to avoid cold, ice, and snow all year round. Friendships are forged with fellow travelers all over the world. Being with the grandkids can be more of a challenge to arrange. No pets are allowed on board. If confined spaces are nerve-wracking, or the thought of living year-round with a spouse or partner is cringeworthy, or worrying if something goes wrong with the home (if renting), then retiring on a ship may not be appealing. Phone calls, TV, and wi-fi may also cost more than what's available on land. If serious illness occurs, the ship's medical staff won't be able to accommodate the illness. Prescription medications are more difficult to refill. If there's a medical emergency, the ship's crew will airlift to the nearest hospital which may or may not be able to handle the situation. Medicare won't cover this, so buy travel insurance that reimburses for air travel to land. If the health scare is serious, don't expect the ship to welcome your loved one back onboard. While in the hospital recuperating, look for housing if the family home was sold before embarking on this adventure. And if the home is rented while overseas, the lease between landlord and tenant will govern when the home will be vacant again. Consider a three-month cruise at first to decide whether this lifestyle is appropriate.

NOTES:

Congregate Care or Independent Living

These facilities offer security without home maintenance. The resident has private living quarters with centralized dining services, shared living spaces, and access to social and recreational activities. Many congregate care facilities offer transportation services, personal care services, rehabilitative services, spiritual programs, and other support services. They can be for independent living, assisted living, Alzheimer's care, or nursing care. This type of housing provides a more intimate setting for your loved one. Its official name is congregate care housing and is a formal arrangement that includes more residents and a staff who provide meals and housekeeping. Also included may be recreation, transportation, and personal care. Residents have their own bedroom within a large house or multifamily home. Most all meals are shared in a central dining area. Residents might also share an everyday living area.

NOTES:

Assisted Living

There may come a day when your loved one can no longer remain in their home. Moving into assisted living is stressful. It's worse if this possibility hasn't been investigated in advance. A fall or other mishap may be the cause of the move there. The sad part occurs when those in charge must make a rush decision on where to move their loved one. Last-minute decisions may have to be based on what is available on short notice, not necessarily on one that the loved one prefers. When a person has trouble performing any of the activities of daily living (ADLs) shown below, he or she may require assisted living where staff is on hand to help with:

- ✔ Bathing
- ✔ Eating
- ✔ Functional mobility (walking, taking stairs)
- ✔ Personal hygiene and grooming (dressing)
- ✔ Toilet hygiene and continence

Here are activities of daily living which are not necessary for fundamental functioning but help your loved one function in a community. They should be able to:

- ✔ Do housework
- ✔ Take medications as prescribed
- ✔ Manage money

✔ Shop for groceries or clothing

✔ Drive/use transportation

✔ Use the telephone

There are more than 30,000 licensed assisted living communities in the US. Assisted living facilities are regulated in all fifty states. All state laws require a resident bill of rights, which should be posted in a conspicuous place. The communities are inspected by the state regulatory agency. Request a copy of their most recent survey report about the community. Assisted living facilities must follow local building codes, fire safety regulations, and more. There should be a resident and family council staff person on hand to address any questions or concerns about the care they provide. Locate the ones closest to where your loved one lives or find ones convenient to where you are if you'll be involved in their care. Each state has its own licensing requirement for this type of facility. Educate yourself in the types of care and services they provide. How large is the entire community, what size apartments are available, what is the monthly cost? Most charge a monthly rent that includes all the services and amenities. A monthly care fee is added to this which is based on how much care the resident needs. They are private pay, which means Medicare doesn't pay for the costs. Payment comes from social security or pensions, the sale of the family home, or other investments. Long-term care insurance can be used, as well as help from family members.

How to Choose an Assisted Living Community That Meets Your Loved One's Needs

Unfortunately, many adult children don't research the care possibilities until it's too late. Their loved one falls, goes into physical therapy to recover, then finds out the home they live in is not designed to move around easily. The better assisted living facilities may or may not have an opening for your loved one when they need to move. Many of the better communities have waitlists.

The National Eldercare Locator administered by the US Administration on Aging (800-677-1116) can help; your local Area Agency/Council on Aging also has resources to help (www. n4a.org). Information is power. Many adult children do not have the time it takes to research the options available, nor do they have the connections to get the best care, nor do they know what questions to ask of a community. The US Department of Health and Human Services provides a list of questions to help you determine whether a facility is right for your loved one (www.bhw.hrsa.gov). Refer to this list of questions as you evaluate the best place for your loved one:

- When you visit, does the lobby appear clean and inviting?

- Did you get a warm greeting from the staff welcoming you?

- Does the person guiding you through the community call residents by name and interact with them as you tour?

- Are you allowed to talk with residents about how they like the community and staff?

- Are residents socializing with one another; are they happy and comfortable?

- Are staff members dressed appropriately, personable, and outgoing?

- Do staff members treat each other in a professional manner?

- What staffing is in place for overnight needs?

- Are visits with your loved one welcomed at any time? If not, why?

- There should be a consumer disclosure form available that discloses personal care and support services, all fees, as well as move-in and move-out provisions.

- What is their policy for refunds and transfers?

- Request and review a residency agreement before moving in.

- Is there a written plan of care for each resident? How often is it reviewed or updated?

- Does the community have a process for assessing a resident's need for services; how often are those needs addressed?

- Does the periodic assessment process include the resident, his or her family, community staff, as well as the resident's physician?

- What are the different costs for various levels or categories of personal care?

- Does the resident need to carry renter's insurance for their personal items in their apartment?

- Ask to see and review the resident bill of rights.

- What is the community's policy on storing medications, help with taking medication, record keeping?

- Is self-administration of medicine allowed?

- Is there a staff person available to coordinate home health-care visits from a nurse, physical therapist, etc. if needed?

- What is the procedure for responding to a resident's medical emergency?

- Is there a nurse on staff?

- Is staff available to provide 24-hour help with ADLs if needed, including dressing, eating, mobility, hygiene and grooming, bathing, and toileting?

- What are the training requirements for staff?

- Are staff required to pass a criminal background check?

- What training is provided to staff in elder abuse and neglect? What is the policy for reporting suspected abuse?

- Does the community allow hospice care?

- Can residents arrange for transportation on short notice?

- Are barbers/beauticians on-site?

- Does the community provide transportation to doctor's offices, hairdressers, shopping, and other activities wanted by residents?

- What type of apartments are available? Floorplans should be available for residents to use for placing furniture they bring from home, etc.

- Do residents have lockable doors in their apartments?

- Is there a twenty-four-hour emergency response system easily accessible inside the apartment?

- Can residents bring their own furnishings? If so, what's allowed? What's provided?

- Does the apartment have phone, cable or satellite TV and internet access? How is billing handled?

- May a resident keep food in their apartment? If so, what kitchen appliances are provided?

- Is smoking permitted?

- Are pets allowed? Is there a size restriction or breed restriction? Only cats or dogs?

- Is there adequate parking for residents and guests?

- Is exterior maintenance, landscaping, and snow removal included in the monthly fee?

- How many floor plan options are available?

- Does each residence have emergency alert and fire suppression systems in place?

- What is available on the menu for breakfast, lunch, dinner? Are snacks available?

- Can the resident request a special diet?

- Can residents eat in their apartments? Are there set times for meals, or can the resident request a special time?

- Can loved ones spend the night and what is the charge?

- What are the reasons a resident is told to move out of a community?

- Request and review the most recent state inspection.

One of the best solutions in making care and placement decisions is to retain the services of an aging life care manager (previously known as a geriatric care manager). Their website is www.aginglifecare.org. Skilled in geriatric social work and nursing care, these experts will guide you through the challenges your loved one may face in their decision making. They can assess the senior's individual needs, prepare comprehensive care plans, and implement those plans. They can be especially helpful if you don't live close to your loved one. Services can include:

- Accompanying your loved one to doctor appointments.

- Coordinate your loved one's care with all others involved, including doctors, family, other caregivers, therapists, nutritionists, elder care attorneys, financial planners, and others.

- Oversee bill paying and managing finances.

- Process paperwork for health insurance coverage, claims, and applications for local, state, or federal benefits.

- Mediate family concerns and conflicts among family members. It's not unusual for a loved one to hesitate talking to you about their health. They may be more willing to share their concerns with a neutral expert outside the family.

- Advocating for the loved one's health care wishes and quality of life.

- Help in choosing the best care facility for your loved one. A care manager understands how these communities work and what the state laws are and can negotiate on your loved one's behalf.

- Care managers are especially helpful if you feel lost or unsure about what to do for your loved one. A care manager can help you understand the options, trade-offs, and costs. And give you peace of mind!

You and your loved one should interview more than one life care manager. Personalities may differ and this person will be working closely with your loved one, so it's important that you both feel comfortable with them and their approach to care. Ask how long they have been in this line of work; they should be able to provide examples of how they customized their care management with other clients. You should also know how they manage emergencies and how they will keep you informed of the progress and condition of your loved one. Ask about payment and how costs for out-of-pocket items are reimbursed. Get everything in writing. Be sure your loved one's doctor advises on the decision. An aging life care manager will often know which facilities have shorter wait lists too.

You may want to evaluate various options on your own. www.APlaceForMom.com is one; others are www.senioradvisor.com, www.caring.com, and www.seniorliving.org. When talking to one of their staff, be sure you understand whether or not the company they provide you with is being paid a referral fee.

Life Plan Community or Continuing Care Retirement Community (CCRC)

Baby Boomers may not want to be told that they are aging, but they may eventually need long-term care, so this option can be adapted to meet their demands. The term continuing care retirement community was re-branded into life plan community, a softer-sounding name that appeals to Baby Boomers, but the care will ultimately be the same or better.

Often the best of all worlds for many, this retirement choice works well for those who want independent living with the knowledge that their future health needs will be met without having to make another major move. To qualify as a life plan community, the community must offer more than one level of care on one campus, focus on promoting an active lifestyle among residents, be socially responsible, and give back to the community at large. These communities are regulated at the state level so Google your state to find out what its definition of life plan community is. Some of these communities are not-for-profit and are often affiliated with faith-based organizations, health systems, universities, or fraternal organizations. People choose this option because they know they will stay there for the duration of their life and be cared for completely. These communities have fitness and/or wellness centers, swimming, activities such as painting or woodworking, dining, and more. There's a significant upfront fee and a monthly fee. Ask about the distinct types of contracts that will make it more affordable for your loved one to live there. Get satisfactory answers to these questions and have a CPA or eldercare attorney review and evaluate the contract before signing:

- ✔ What types of contracts are offered?

  1. Type A contracts provide overall housing, residential services and amenities, and unlimited health care services. Future costs are more predictable, but residents pay a larger entrance fee. The monthly fee is flat for all levels of care.

  2. Type B is a modified agreement. Type B will also include housing and residential services. But Type B doesn't cover all future healthcare needs. This type of plan does offer discounted rates for those services. If an increase in care becomes necessary, the resident is responsible for covering the extra costs.

  3. Type C contracts cover housing, residential services, and health care. It's more of a pay-as-you-go. Residents pay a lower entrance fee at the beginning. If you don't need higher levels of care, there won't be an additional cost to you beyond your monthly service fee for amenities. Yes, the resident will save up front on costs, but the potential risk for larger costs may be much higher, depending on the need.

- ✔ There are usually three types of entrance fees that are structured this way:

  1. Declining scale refunds or amortizing entrance fees. This type specifies a period in which the entrance fee is refundable, on a declining basis. For example, if the entrance fee declines at the rate of one percent each

month, then after 6 months 94 percent of the entrance fee would be refundable.

2. Partially refundable entrance fees guarantee a specific percentage of the refund that will be returned within a certain period, regardless of how long the resident has been there. An example would be a refundable 50 percent of the entrance fee if the resident passes away.

3. The third option is a full refund of the entrance fee. A fixed charge will likely be deducted before the refund is made and the agreement should state how long the refund is valid and under what conditions a refund is due. These entrance fees are usually more expensive than those without the options in numbers one and two.

Here are questions to ask:

+   What's the ratio of independent living residences to assisted living and skilled care? As your loved one ages, it's important to be sure that there will be a place for them without having to go to another facility for care.

+   What health care costs are covered in the agreement the resident will sign? What costs are paid out-of-pocket?

+   Are there any tax advantages with a CCRC? What percentage of the entrance fee and monthly service fee can be deducted from a tax return?

+   What is the entrance fee? Is it affordable? Their staff will evaluate the loved one's financial ability to pay.

- How long can they keep their apartment in the independent living section if they require skilled nursing care for a period in another part of the community? How much extra will it cost?

- What happens if dad requires care in another area of the CCRC, but mom doesn't? What's the cost for mom to stay in an independent apartment and what happens if one of them requires longer care in assisted living?

- Is the entrance fee partially or fully refundable? How much is refunded and over what period? How long does it take to get the refund?

- What's the monthly fee and what does it cover? How much has the monthly fee increased in the past few years? Is there a plan for your loved one if they can't pay the higher fee?

- How is the community managed? How long have the staff been there? What kind of training and continuing education does the staff have? How long have the top-level executives been there?

- Are residents allowed to have input into the decision-making process?

- Is there a waitlist? Many people make the decision to move into a smaller apartment and move up once they're residents. When units become available, current residents are often given a "first choice" over those who are still on the outside waiting list.

- Does your loved one give up any legal rights when they move in? If so, what are they?

- How are the meals? Will the chef accommodate their needs if they have a special diet? Can the resident choose which time they want to eat? How dressed up does a resident have to be to eat in the dining room? Can a resident take their meal back to their apartment or do they have to eat in the dining room?

- Is there a housekeeping service? Is the cost included or is it an extra fee? If so, how much does it cost?

- Is parking included? If not, what is the monthly fee for one space? More than one space?

- Are pets allowed? Are pets pre-screened to see how they adapt to the new living environment?

- Under what conditions might they be asked to move out of their apartment? Who makes that final decision? What are the conditions that must be met for a move?

- Can family members stay on-site for a weekend visit? If so, how much does it cost?

- Is transportation provided to go grocery shopping? Is the grocery store transport only offered on a certain day of the week? Which stores are included on the list?

- What plans are in place for dealing with natural or human-caused disasters?

- What plan is in place if the Office of Emergency Preparedness declares a shelter-in-place emergency? How will evacuation to an off-site shelter be handled? How will relatives be notified?

- Who decides whether and when the resident must move to a higher level of care? Can a family member hire a private duty care provider above and beyond what the facility provides?

- What type of activities are available? Which are free and which cost extra? Is there an activities director? Are the residents allowed to give input as to the type of activities they would like?

- Review the financial status of the community. This is particularly important!

- If the resident dies or leaves, does the resident have to pay the monthly fee for their apartment until a new resident is found?

- What technology is available? This would include cable TV, Internet access, and Wi-Fi, as well as a central computer room where they could either take lessons in computer use or access online sites such as e-mail or Facebook.

- There are communities that promise to pay up to a certain amount towards moving expenses. Be aware that this cost comes out of the Realtor's® pocket. These communities provide names of Realtors® who can help you through the process of moving. These Realtors® must agree in writing to give a fee to the community in exchange for the lead. If you have a favorite Realtor® you want to use instead, find out what provisions, if any, are made for moving expenses.

+ Before signing any contract, consult with a financial advisor. Research the organization to determine its financial stability and quality level of management. Be certain to understand what is and isn't covered in the contract. What role can your family members play. If the resident's condition changes, can that information be shared with a trusted friend or family member?

NOTES:

Advantages of Moving to a Location Nearby

✔ The same doctors are close by and friends too (unless they move!) but they no longer have maintenance or upkeep on the home.

✔ Downsize to a smaller space. Widowed or divorced may welcome the opportunity to minimize their space.

✔ Or upsize! There are Baby Boomers with large or blended families and need a space large enough to accommodate everyone who visits!

✔ Have all primary living space on one level.

It may be better to sell the family home and rent for a while. Although this means moving twice, renting provides an opportunity to explore all options. If the budget allows, list the home for rent when you move to a new location. The rental income can often help offset the cost of the new home. Consult with a CPA to learn the tax implications of absentee ownership.

NOTES:

Downsizing/De-cluttering Tips

Start early to sort through their belongings! They don't want the pressure of making quick decisions on personal belongings at the last minute. It can be overwhelming to think of sorting through the entire house, so start small. Sort through one or two drawers in the kitchen or do one closet per day. Here is a guide to use in deciding what to take and what to sell:

- ✔ Obtain the floor plan of the new home and measure their existing furniture to see what will fit in the new space. If an old sofa is too difficult to sit on, buy a new one and have it delivered to the new home. This decision can also be used for buying a new mattress.

- ✔ Decide what to keep, what to sell, and what will be given away or thrown out. The IRS allows $500 per year for charitable donations without an appraisal. If an appraisal is done for more expensive treasures, more can be deducted. Consult with a CPA to decide how to proceed under IRS guidelines.

- ✔ Compare the cost of moving existing furniture with the cost of buying new furniture for the new location. It is likely that moving from a colder climate to a warmer one, that leather sofa in the living room may not feel as comfortable in a warmer climate. There is a thrift store on every other corner in Florida which displays donated pieces that newcomers insisted on bringing with them and find they are not needed.

- ✔ Decide how to dispose of unwanted items. Items can be sold on eBay, Craigslist, or through an auction house, consignment shop, estate sale, or online sale.

✔ If family or friends want certain items, then the items should be picked up well ahead of time. If they do not pick up the items, have the items hauled away. **Then Do It!**

Behind the Scenes: I worked with a client who needed to sell her 5,000-square-foot home in an upscale neighborhood. Although she lived alone in the home, it was filled with clothes and other items she had bought from a TV shopping network. She was obsessed with buying things she didn't need to fill a void that would always be empty. If your loved one has a compulsion to buy this way, call the shopping network staff and have them freeze the credit card so purchases cannot be made.

Behind the Scenes: An older couple finally learned that the apartment they wanted was going to be available soon. They called to let me know that it was time to get serious about packing and moving. My home inspector had completed an inspection and the items that needed fixing were completed. I had the roof inspected by my trusted roofer so I knew that would not be an issue. I talked with the wife of the couple about how to start paring down the items to take. She had four complete services for twelve of china that she brought out at Christmas, Thanksgiving, July Fourth, and any other special occasion she felt called for their use. She couldn't take all the china with her since they would be eating most meals in the community's dining room. She had saved about a dozen Styrofoam cups from a fast-food restaurant. One of my Team members started to throw them out because they were old and worn out. She said "NO! Those are the cups my husband uses to soak his dentures in!" She finally agreed to switch them for a small glass bowl he could use for the same purpose.

Moving Tips That Will Save
You Money and Stress

✔ Hire quality movers. Obtain estimates from reputable local companies. Make a list of what each service the company supplies and ask if their estimate includes reassembling furniture or installing appliances. The move estimator will ask if there's easy access to the new home (is it down a winding dirt road, up a steep hill, or an asphalt driveway?). If your loved ones are moving to a building with an elevator, the move estimator needs to know what floor the unit is on and how far away the entry door is from the elevator (this determines how many people are needed to load and unload). Always research the company carefully, read the reviews, and ask others for recommendations. Insist on an in-home estimate so their quote is as exact as possible. Spending a little more to hire a quality company will be cheaper than firing a moving company if the move doesn't go as planned, or if they lose belongings, or if the mover is a scammer (a mover may quote one price before the move, then refuse to unload unless more is paid than originally agreed upon). And, under no circumstances should your loved one try to load a moving van on their own! I have watched in horror as sixty-year-olds pack the U-Haul and hurt their back so that unpacking on the other end is nearly impossible.

✔ Try to move during the 'off' season. Summer is the busiest moving season. If there is flexibility when planning the move, schedule it between September and May. Moving companies are in the most demand on the first and last few days of any month. The cost of the move depends on how far away the new location is, how much the belongings weigh, and the cost to pack and unpack.

✔ De-clutter! Why pay a mover to pack and move items no longer needed? It's too expensive and unnecessary. Sell, donate, or give away items that have outlived their usefulness or are not needed. Moving sales, charity donations (save receipts for tax purposes), or auctions and estate sales are effective ways to dispose of items.

✔ While sorting through belongings, take pictures or make a video of special items, not only for insurance purposes but also to record memories for future generations. The pictures of donated items help in preparing tax returns as well.

✔ Keep all receipts. Some moving expenses may be tax-deductible. If the move is due to a job, some of the expense may be written off when itemizing tax returns. A CPA can advise on the matter.

✔ Pack some items separately. Items like books (use small boxes to avoid too much weight) and non-fragile items can be packed separately, by friends or family. This not only saves money but also allows for donating the books no longer needed. If the boxes are not packed by the movers, mark the box "PBO" (Packed by Owner) on the outside. It's best to have the movers pack fragile items; that way, the mover is fully responsible for breakage.

✔ Look for hidden fees. Always read the fine print when hiring a mover. There may be fees such as insurance or random fees that the company will add as junk fees. Ask questions if there is something that is not clear.

✔ Will more than one car need transporting? Use trusted drivers or a car transport service. If it's an east coast move to Florida, consider packing the vehicle with immediate-need items and use the auto train to travel.

✔ Don't forget pets! Transporting them safely can be stressful for them. Discuss options with the veterinarian. Don't forget to check on licenses for pets in the new location.

✔ Change the address online with the US Post Office (www. usps.gov) . Notify the change of address with banks, friends, doctors, insurance company, and family members. Recurring subscriptions like magazines will need four to six weeks' notice to change an address.

✔ Obtain a driver's license in the new location if your loved one can still drive. Register vehicles at the new motor vehicle location.

✔ Register to vote in the new location. Set up new bank accounts.

NOTES:

Selling the Family Home

This is a big step for any owner. Due to the many variables involved, hire a Realtor® who has experience in handling this type of sale. Your neighbor's best friend's uncle who hasn't managed a transaction like this is not going to be of help. An experienced Realtor® will have trusted resources to help you as well and can handle the logistics of the sale. Memories and emotions can overtake rational decisions. Many of my clients have lived in their homes for twenty-five to sixty years and it's hard to give up the familiar for something new. It means sorting through years of accumulated belongings. There are options to consider when selling. One option is to fix up the house and sell it for top dollar. A second option is to sell AS IS and do nothing except clean up and arrange furniture so buyers can easily access the rooms in the house.

A third option is to sell to an investor for a low price. The investor handles cleaning out the contents of the house. If this route is chosen, understand that you won't be getting a market price. Be sure to find and remove any important documents ahead of the sale.

> ✔ **Preparation:** Once your loved one decides to move, they need to act as though the house is no longer their own. Yes, there are memories and those can be captured and preserved. But, depending on the market conditions, the home may need to be prepared for today's buyers, so understanding what those buyers want is critical. Will they sell the home in AS IS condition or refurbish it to sell? Deciding what to keep, what to sell, and what to give away is an emotional decision (See more details under De-cluttering). Retirees may think they need to

make major changes to their home to sell. Big-ticket improvements should be left to the Buyer. Depending on the market, a Realtor® may recommend these effective improvements that make a house attractive to a potential buyer:

✔ If the house is not sold "AS IS," consider completing a pre-listing home inspection by an inspector who is licensed and a member of ASHI (American Society of Home Inspectors). The Realtor® will be able to give the owner the names of reputable inspectors or they can choose someone licensed that has been referred to them. Many times, during an inspection, deferred maintenance issues will arise that were overlooked, done improperly, or postponed. Once the inspector prepares a list of issues that might arise, take a proactive approach and fix the higher-cost tasks prior to listing the property. Buyers like to make offers on properties that have been well cared for.

✔ Paint inside and out where needed.

✔ Deep-clean the house.

✔ Change tired countertops for a fresh look (no, granite is not needed to sell unless it is a higher-priced listing).

✔ Expose hardwood floors under the carpet whenever possible. Better yet, remove the carpet whenever possible to expose any hardwood flooring underneath. If this is not possible, pull back a corner of the carpet to show what's underneath.

✔ Update the faucets in the kitchen and baths.

✔ Improve lighting (inside and out; even something low-cost like replacing lightbulbs will brighten a room).

✔ Install new appliances.

✔ Power-wash the exterior.

✔ De-clutter the home. Buyers are not buying the furnishings, artwork, or collections. They want a simple floor plan with an easy flow throughout the house. They can't get a feel for what it would be like to live there if cluttered rooms are preventing them from visualizing the space. Millennials are ages twenty-seven to forty-two and they won't have accumulated as many belongings as a long-time owner has. Too many personal items on display can make them cross your home off their list.

✔ Stage the property. Your Realtor® can recommend staging the house prior to taking photos. Depending on circumstances, the existing furniture can be arranged attractively, or new pieces brought in from a professional stager. The home will appear at its best on the internet when the furniture is arranged in a welcoming way. Costs to stage will depend on the location and price point for the property as well as square footage. Some companies allow payment at settlement instead of upfront. Virtual staging is also used with the disclosure online that shows a photo of the empty room and then followed by a photo of the room virtually staged with furniture.

The home should have a fresh, clean look so that B-buyers can move right in and start living there at once. If improvements are made upfront, the owner will reap the return. Or sell AS IS and walk away with less. If you are targeting primarily Millennials (those born in the mid-'80s to late '90s), you may need to make improvements that will appeal to that age group. A photoshoot/virtual tour that appeals to them is a necessity. They grew up using smart phones and apps. They communicate through text and video. They like smaller homes on smaller lots, so price the home accordingly and understand that they don't want to deal with upkeep. They prefer living close to urban areas. An accomplished Realtor® will target the buyer for the home, whether it's a first-time buyer or a move-up buyer who needs more space, and market the home accordingly.

- ✔ **Price:** The price will depend on the selling prices of other properties nearby that have been sold recently. The price will also depend on the time of year, the location of the home, and how many other properties are competing with it at the time it is listed. Decide either to invest money in making improvements and ask for a better price, or not to spend money and settle for a lower price. There is a wider audience of buyers who prefer to buy something in "move-in" condition than there are buyers who buy to make the improvements themselves (often investors). Do not make the mistake of using Zillow to decide the list price. They are not licensed appraisers and do not follow federal regulations. Remember that if your home needs $50,000 or more to update it, don't expect to get the same price as the neighbor who updated all the baths and remodeled their kitchen.

- ✔ **Promotion:** Pro-active marketing strategies are used to attract buyers to their home instead of the homes competing with it. Excellent professional photos, virtual tours, videos, 3-D tours, can supply a good social media campaign and are a few of the avenues available through your Realtor®. The use of drones to shoot overhead views of the property and surrounding areas is popular, too. (As of August 2016, drone usage is restricted to companies that meet FAA requirements.) The largest audience is composed of first-time buyers who tend to be younger and do not have experience in making home improvements. However, they are savvy users of technology and will shop for a home online.

When Fixing Up to Sell the Family Home Is Not the Best Solution

Sometimes heirs cannot agree on how to dispose of the family home. Selling AS IS, renting the home, or having one sibling buy out the others are other options.

Selling AS IS: If there has been hoarding in the home, it may be best to sell to an investor who will be responsible for removing the contents of the house, as well as the cost of fixing it up or tearing it down and building a new home in its place. The owner will not get as much for the property but will not have the stress of buyers, inspectors, and appraisers coming through while the house is on the market. If there is enough value in the contents, an online auction can be done to sell items that are worth something. The proceeds can be used to offset moving costs.

Renting: If the home is in decent shape, the heirs may decide to paint and fix it up to rent. The income from the monthly rental can offset the cost of the new place, whether it be assisted living or some other type of care. The owner will still have to maintain the property and verify that the potential renters are credit-worthy. Consult a CPA on the tax limitations of this type of arrangement.

Buying Out the Other Heirs: If one of the heirs has been living in the house while caring for their parent(s), he or she may want to stay. This is a possibility, provided the other heirs agree to receive their portion of cash at settlement. An appraisal of the house value must be done to determine the selling price. And the heir buying the others out must have the income needed to take on a mortgage for that amount if they don't have the cash to buy out the others. They also need to carry any outstanding mortgage, insurance, utilities, and taxes. **NOTE:** If the sibling who has been caring for mom and dad has been living in the home, they may not want to move. If this issue cannot be resolved satisfactorily, it may require filing a partition lawsuit with the probate court to sell the home. Consult an estate or elder law attorney for details in your state.

Selling to an Investor or Selling the Home Yourself: Desperate situations require desperate measures. Investor purchasers will give you a "low-ball" offer and prey on the elder's emotions. They will also allow them to leave behind all the "stuff" left in a hoarder property. While this will save money, this same approach can be achieved by selling "AS IS." Selling the home without representation is not a wise idea. The owners are too emotionally wrapped up in the memories of living there. And the investor isn't representing you! An experienced Realtor® will guide you throughout the selling process and advise on the best way to get the greatest return.

Settlement Tips: Since the property had previous owners, the settlement company or attorney will request a copy of the owner's death certificates, a copy of the will, and, if the property is deeded to a trust, a copy of the trust that shows who the trustee is and that they have the power to sell property in the trust. Often a summary page and the notary page are enough to provide but be sure you have access to all pages, just in case. The settlement company will also need any death certificates if an owner has died. A form of ID, usually a driver's license, is needed if the person is still living and signing the settlement documents. A document is provided at the settlement that shows all the expenses involved in selling the home. These could include unpaid taxes, outstanding mortgage, local and state fees charged by the district or state where the property is found. If the house was professionally staged, the fee will appear on the form and be subtracted from the final proceeds. There may be other fees or charges as well, depending on the jurisdiction. The settlement attorney will review these and explain the charges. If you're signing on behalf of your loved one, you will supply the documentation that gives you the power to sign on their behalf if they are still living. If they have passed, proof of executorship or administrator is needed. Some states have attorneys to oversee the transaction completely. Other states provide that a settlement company or attorney can manage the transaction. Your Realtor® will explain this to you ahead of time. Choose your Realtor® carefully. She or he should have considerable experience in estate and trust property sales to guide you through this process.

NOTES:

Live or Age in Place in *Their* Home

As of October 2021, approximately 10.5 million homes in the US were between 20 and 31 years old. Those dwellings were not built with aging in place in mind. Americans are living longer, and mobility and eyesight decline with age. Safety issues become a factor in staying at home (narrow hallways, slippery floors, unsafe bathrooms, too many steps to access the house from the outside, poor lighting, kitchens that are a challenge to use, etc.) Some homes can be retrofitted to accommodate the changes that can improve the safety of the property; others cannot because of the way they are constructed. A well-designed home (or addition) allows the resident to move around safely, use the bathroom and bedroom safely, and perform daily activities with little or no help.

Aging in place, or living in place, allows your loved one to stay in their own home safely and independently. The goal is to live comfortably, regardless of income or ability to function. The home can be retrofitted to accommodate their future needs or an addition to the house can be constructed, which achieves this goal as well. Aging or living in place allows your loved one to keep their doctors, use the neighborhood amenities which they are familiar with, and, unless they decide to move, keep their friends and neighbors. Aging in place may not work for everyone, and it won't be the final solution. If the decision to stay in the home is what seems best for now, you'll still need to explore other options since failing health will cause issues in the future that may require moving into a facility. Get on the wait lists of communities that your loved ones like. An emergency or crisis is not the time to look for a place to go for care. And the place that your loved one likes may not have an opening. **Don't Wait Until It's Too Late!**

Many people over fifty-five want to stay in their home and adapt it to their needs. The goal of aging in place is to enhance the quality of life. This is an admirable goal but will require spending money to remodel (especially in older homes) and making provisions for ongoing care. Aging in place may include widening hallways and doorways; adding a shaftless elevator or chair lift which enables the owner to move about inside freely (be careful about installing a chair lift or stair lift; if a paramedic can't easily access a higher floor with a gurney to rescue someone with a heart attack or fall emergency, then time is lost.) Remodeling the kitchen so counters are easier to reach, and appliances made more accessible may be needed as well. The costs can outweigh the benefits for many in adapting a house to include universal design features. Another big issue is the deferred maintenance that arises from neglecting tasks over time. Older owners often have limited vision and may not readily see damage from mold or water leakage, termite infestation, and the like. They also tend to accumulate things and are hesitant to clean out their home to improve their safety. A home inspection should be completed to decide what, if anything, should be done to make the house safe to age in place. Cleaning out the house so that it becomes safe to walk through and use comfortably is important. In addition to remodeling, there are costs involved in onsite medical care. It is a good idea to plan for space to allow for a live-in care provider.

A care companion can help relieve the stress of family members who otherwise provide onsite care. Some agencies employ or contract with nurses and other skilled labor to spend time with your loved one and help around the house. The advantage of this more expensive alternative is that the workers are pre-screened, so you do not have to conduct a background check on your own. There are various levels of care which include a care companion who handles interacting and watching your loved one on a regular basis. They can provide transportation, meal preparation, and housekeeping. A home health aide is someone who will help with bathing, toileting, and dressing. A registered nurse provides more intense care such as administering medication, treating wounds, and taking blood pressure and pulse regularly. If you are hiring a person to care for your loved one, you can contact nursing schools, social work students at a local college, or reach out to your area agency on aging for recommendations. At first, you can expect your loved one to resist a stranger in their home. But once they interact with the new person, they enjoy it. Social interaction is valuable. You will need to provide details on the care companion's duties. Do you need them to be companions? Run errands? Do light housekeeping? Take them on outings? Be sure to check their employment record and references as well as their driving record. You may want to hire someone from a company that specializes in background checks. Some Medicare Advantage plans cover such care. And check the long-term care policy to see if this type of service is provided.

NOTES:

Questions to Ask in Deciding Whether Your Loved One Can Age Where They Are

✔ Can they maintain the home comfortably? Do they have trusted contractors who can mow the lawn, clean the gutters, paint as needed, service the HVAC, and complete similar tasks? Proper care of the home lowers the chances of major problems or costly repairs later. Even simple tasks like changing the sheets or replacing a light bulb in a ceiling fixture can be a challenge.

✔ Does the home have the safety features they need to age in place? For example, are doorways wide enough to accommodate a wheelchair or walker? Is the entrance to the home stair-free? According to the Centers for Disease Control and Prevention, thirty million older adults fall every single year, making it the top cause of injury and death in this age group. And the chances of falling a second time doubled. One out of five falls causes severe injury, e.g., head injury or broken bones. Bathrooms are one of the places where falls occur most often. Install a taller toilet with a flushing attachment to help in caring for your loved one. If your loved one insists on installing a step-in tub with a door that locks and they can sit on a bench to take a bath, be sure they understand that they must sit in the tub and wait for the tub to fill. When they finish bathing, they must wait for the tub to drain. They cannot get out until the water is drained and there is no way for a care provider to access them if there's an emergency until the tub has drained. Crucial time may be lost.

✔ Do the doors have lever handles instead of knobs to make them easier to open? There are more issues that need to be addressed for them to live safely at home. Older homes do not have kitchens and baths equipped to handle the needs of seniors. A contractor who specializes in the needs of people who want to age in place can help solve these problems.

✔ Would a move improve their lifestyle? Moving closer to family, moving to a warmer climate, or owning a new home with safety features already built in are some of the reasons people over the age of fifty-five move.

✔ Can they use the equity in their home for improvements? There are options for obtaining the funds to make the improvements. One is a HELOC (home equity line of credit). Another is a HECM (home equity conversion mortgage) or reverse mortgage. A third possibility is the HECM for Purchase, which makes it easier for older homeowners to downsize or move to another area. A reverse mortgage allows them to stay in their home. They still own it, but they are using the equity to make improvements. Be sure to read the fine print and discuss the terms with an attorney before signing any loan papers.

✔ Are there funds for at-home care? They may need an aide to visit regularly to help with everyday tasks, or they may need the service of an aging life care manager (formerly known as a geriatric care manager) to supervise and direct their care. A care manager ensures that medication is taken, doctor visits are made, and any follow-up is completed. The value of working with an aging life care manager is that they have a wealth of knowledge in caring for your parent, they have resources and advocates who approach care holistically, they can mediate conflict and provide crisis intervention, provide referrals for essential resources, and so much more.

✔ Is the home suited for having another person (e.g., a caregiver) live there as well? It's often necessary to make improvements to the home to accommodate an in-home care provider.

✔ Is your loved one willing to incorporate technology and products that help them remain safely in their home longer while providing family caregivers peace of mind? There are many options available now, and with the use of artificial intelligence (AI) on the rise, many more will be designed to help people age in place. Technology can help your loved one by providing mental stimulation (think sudoku puzzle, online crossword, learning through a YouTube video, etc.). Technology can diminish the feeling of isolation by increasing outside contact with friends and family through FaceTime or other video chat. There are message boards and groups for people with common interests that can provide a sense of community while staying in their home. Smartphones, fitness watches, apps that remind a person to take their medication, schedule a doctor's appointment, and so much more. If your loved one has mobility or vision issues, groceries can be delivered to them via online shopping. Ride-sharing apps can pick them up and drop them off at the grocery store or mall. There are voice-activated technologies which allow people to turn on music or raise the temperature using verbal commands. Personal monitoring devices have GPS functions and other alert systems, such as fall detection, which provide peace of mind to family as well as their loved ones. Each year, the Consumer Electronics Show (CES) holds its trade show in Las Vegas (usually in January). There you will find the latest technology for the older adult.

✔ It is important to talk with your loved one to figure out the issues that may be present. Do they forget to take medications? Is there enough lighting? Are there balance issues that may lead to a fall? Safety, security, and privacy are the key elements in deciding which products may help them age in place safely. If the product doesn't provide value, then they're not likely to use it. Baby Boomer parents are quite able to adapt to technology if cost and usefulness are also taken into consideration. Video cameras, motion sensor lighting, smartphone apps like Alexa Together, Google, or Apple Home can provide the caregiver with the ability to track health status and their routine.

NOTES:

Create a Safe Space

One out of four people over the age of sixty-five fall each year. Falls are the leading cause of injury-related deaths for those over the age of sixty-five (https://www.cdc.gov) Here are a range of improvements that can and should be made to ease the stress of aging in place. Many people wait until an emergency happens before they get the help they need.

Do This Before It's Too Late:

✔ Install lever handles on the interior doors and faucet handles to replace knobs.

✔ Improve lighting throughout the interior and exterior of the home. **The outside light near the house number should be bright enough to be easily seen by an ambulance. The house numbers should be large enough to easily see from the street.** Switch to a brighter bulb on lamps or, at the very least, wipe the dust from existing bulbs to improve the light.

✔ There should be a full bath, bedroom, and kitchen access on the main level. There may be a half-bath that could be expanded to include a low threshold shower with a hand-held unit and a built-in bench. Non-skid mats in a bathroom shower are an added benefit. A seventeen to nineteen inch toilet that sits higher on the floor will make it easier to use, especially if it has washing capabilities. Non-slip flooring is also important. **Note for walk-in bathtubs:** The bather must get in the tub and sit while the tub fills with water and must remain in the tub until the water drains. It can take seven to ten minutes to fill a tub and fifteen minutes to drain. The cost depends on the features needed, such as a heated seat, handrails, slip-resistant floors, rapid draining, or a rapid call system in case of emergency. The cost ranges from $2,000-$20,000 depending on the features chosen and the age of the plumbing and other factors. **Because of the design, it is harder for a caregiver to help with bathing an older adult.** Without a built-in call button or rapid drain system, the bather must wait for the water to drain before exiting the tub. Minutes are lost trying to call 9-1-1 in case of a medical emergency. The door needs to be latched properly since the weight of the water can force it open and flooding will occur.

✔ Many colonial-style homes weren't built to convert a half-bath on the main level; often an addition is built to meet the need. Chairlifts or stairlifts may be necessary. Compare the cost of buying it vs renting a lift before you decide which one to choose.

✔ Interior doorways should be thirty-six inches wide (to allow for wheelchairs and walkers or the presence of a companion).

✔ The hallways should be forty-two inches wide.

✔ The carpet, if any, should be tightly woven, low-pile, and smooth. Remove scatter rugs, which can move and trigger a fall.

✔ Grab bars should be installed where needed (be sure to add extra support behind the wall). These are often in the shower area and next to the toilet.

✔ Stairways need secure handrails on either side.

✔ Install smoke and carbon monoxide detectors near the bedrooms. Follow your local fire code instructions.

✔ Replace toggle light switches with rocker panel switches to make it easier to turn on lights.

✔ If outside steps are an issue, a ramp can be constructed that does not look like a ramp. Walkways should be at least thirty-six inches wide.

✔ Include technology in a renovation or remodel.

NOTES:

Remodeling Tips for Small or Large Projects

If your loved ones want to age in place where they are or you need to modify your own home before your loved ones can move in with you, there are some decisions to be made. When should you use an architect? When should you use a design-build firm? When is a general contractor sufficient? A design-build firm is a general contractor with a designer, architect, or engineer in-house. An architect works for an independent firm who works for you as the client. The architect prepares plans and gets the necessary permits for construction. Once the permit is in hand, the owner then hires a contractor to build the project. If you're doing a major re-design (knocking out walls or other structural issues) and you're concerned about the aesthetics of the final look, then an architect is the way to go. The advantage of a design-build team is that all these services are under one roof and the builder helps manage the cost, so you stay within your budget. A general contractor can do a simple bathroom or kitchen remodel of an existing space and will be less expensive. Regardless of which one you choose; be sure you understand what services will be provided (called a scope of work) and that the company has extensive experience in doing the kind of work that needs to be done. Be sure you research to confirm that the company you choose is insured against negligence or malpractice and conforms with your state's licensing requirements. A design-build firm will show you a limited choice of finishes (tile, faucets, kitchen cabinets, etc.) They will give you a budget allowance and you won't be able to send the project out for bid with another company.

A contractor or architect or design-build firm specializing in aging in place solutions can be called upon to help you further. At the very least, the firm should have at least one Certified Aging in Place Specialist® (CAPS) team member. The National Association of Homebuilders provides certification for builders and others in the housing field who specialize in universal design. The graduates hold the Certified Aging in Place Specialist (CAPS) designation. These professionals will meet with you and discuss your day-to-day needs as well as the future. I hold the CAPS® designation and have worked to create aging in place space for families who want to include parents in their space. Many of the homes I inspected were built with doorways too narrow, hallways that cannot accommodate a walker or wheelchair or even an aide walking next to the person, small bathrooms, and steps that don't allow the older adult to navigate safely.

NOTES:

Can a Reverse Mortgage Be Used to Pay for Renovations?

If your loved one is over the age of sixty-two, and has equity in the home, he or she should consider using this program to remain in their home and make improvements. One of the most common types of reverse mortgages is the Home Equity Conversion Mortgage (HECM). It's insured by the Federal Housing Administration, a part of the US Department of Housing and Urban Development (HUD). If there is an existing mortgage on their home, the reverse mortgage proceeds are used to pay off that loan and the balance can be used for other purposes. They will no longer make payments on their home. A reverse mortgage allows them to take the money as a line of credit, a lump sum, monthly payments over a set length of time, or payments apportioned over the rest of their life. There are stipulations that homeowners must follow:

1. Their home must be their principal residence (they must live there for more than 6 months of the year).

2. They must own the home free and clear, or the existing mortgage is so low that it can be paid off with the proceeds of the reverse mortgage.

3. They can't owe any federal debt (like back taxes or student loans). Keep in mind that the money from the reverse mortgage can be used to pay those off.

4. Your loved one must have enough monthly income to pay property taxes and insurance as well as maintenance and repair costs.

5. The home must be in good condition. If it is not, the lender will tell them what repairs need to be made to qualify for the loan.

6. Your loved ones must attend a counseling session from a HUD (Housing and Urban Development)-approved reverse mortgage counseling agency. The counselor will discuss with your loved ones the financial implications of the loan as well as their eligibility.

Their home cannot be taken away from them as long as they pay the taxes, insurance, utilities, and upkeep on it. They will never owe more than the home's value at the time the loan is repaid, even if they received more than the value of their home. The money they receive is tax-free too. Be aware that many owners think the upfront fees are too high even though the fees can be rolled into the reverse mortgage. If they do not continue to pay the taxes and insurance and fail to live in their home for more than six months of the year, they can lose their home to foreclosure. As an heir to their estate, you may inherit less, or even nothing, of the value of your parents' home. This type of mortgage requires that their home be sold within a certain time after their death. It's important that they discuss this choice with their financial advisor and/or their elder law attorney to understand all the aspects of this type of mortgage. It may be that this solution would solve the problem of remodeling the home to age in place by providing adequate funds to do so.

Live or Age in Place In *Your* Home

According to the AARP's Policy Institute and the National Alliance for Caregiving's publication *Caregiving in the United States 2020*, in 2010 there were more than seven potential family caregivers for every person over eighty; by 2030, that ratio is expected to fall to four to one; by 2050, there will be fewer than three to one. More care responsibilities will fall on fewer family members, most of them adult children. The decision to move your loved one into your home can be challenging and stressful. In addition to the cost of adapting existing space so it's safe, you may need to give up leisure time and time with your children, not to mention the added stress to your well-being. There's non-stop laundry, meal planning and preparation, as well as grocery shopping for an extra person or two. If your loved one is becoming forgetful, you'll need to monitor their pill-taking. You'll also be responsible for overseeing their medical bills. Younger people who are not used to dealing with complex health situations may become anxious dealing with filling out paperwork, etc.

It may help your schedule if your loved one is under the same roof, even though it may be more stressful. Checking on them, taking them where they need to go, etc. may be easier than traveling regularly to their home. Your loved ones may not want to admit that they need more attentive care and assisted living costs make that possibility out of the question. The interaction of grandchildren with a grandparent is often a benefit too. Older grandchildren can take on many tasks in helping. Boundaries need to be set up so that privacy is respected. If both adult children work full-time, then the care your loved one needs, and the cost involved, may be more than you can handle. Placing a dollar value on unpaid care provided (mostly by daughters) is complicated. And the added stress needs to be considered as well. A caregiver may be a choice for solving this time problem if funds permit. If you decide to hire a caregiver, you'll want to be sure a background check was done on the person providing care and you should expect the following tasks to be part of the checklist. The tasks will depend on what your loved ones need, what they want, and what emergency plans you will put in place, such as where emergency supplies are in the home, an emergency contact, and more. You'll need to create a list of names, addresses, and phone numbers of your loved one's doctors, and other family members as well as their medications and dosages. You will need to know their bank accounts, insurance policies, their social security number, insurance card, and other important personal information. Your caregiver list will need to adhere to HIPPA (Health Insurance Portability and Accountability Act). If this information is digital, be sure the platform you use is secure and that only authorized users can access it.

Your caregiver checklist should be tailored to your loved one's needs and wishes. Consider these tasks and include them, depending on what you can do and what the caregiver should do, and what your loved ones want:

Medical: Check their vital signs (including blood sugar and blood pressure), schedule and transport them to doctor visits or other medical appointments. They may need to be reminded to take their medication. If prescriptions are taken, someone will need to pick them up from the pharmacy or arrange to have them delivered by mail.

Personal: A caregiver should be able to help with bathing, washing, and styling hair, brushing their teeth, shaving, trimming nails, getting dressed, and changing sheets.

Nutrition: It is most likely that you'll shop for groceries for your loved one and prepare their meals and, when needed, help with feeding. But the caregiver you hire should be willing to complete these tasks if needed. If you shop at bulk stores, you can set aside some of the staple items for your loved one to use.

Toileting: The caregiver should be ready to help with going to the bathroom, assist with a bedpan or urinal if used, and empty a catheter or colonoscopy bag. Installing a taller toilet with a washing attachment will provide a way to deal with this concern. If your loved one wants to take a bath and you decide to install a step-in bathtub, remember that they must first get in and close the door tightly. Then they wait for the water to fill to the desired depth. Once they finish bathing, they must wait for the water to drain out of the tub first before they can open the door and get out. Supervision may be needed!

Mobility: Family members or a caregiver can assist with walking, helping your loved one get in and out of bed, and assisting with home exercises that are right for your loved one.

Household chores: Include changing the sheets in this list as well. Often, a parent loses strength in their ability to bend over or has arthritis that prevents them from changing the sheets easily. Laundering the sheets should be completed by a family member or caregiver. Light housekeeping can be done on a regular basis as well as emptying the trash. Depending on the person you hire, they may also pay bills, unless that is a task that a responsible family member can do for them.

Interaction with your loved one: If no family member is available, the caregiver can take your loved one on a walk, drive them to appointments (check their driving history), read aloud to them, play games, or simply have meaningful conversation. The caregiver can monitor the schedule and duration of guest visits and friends or enroll them in learning activities like painting or cooking or crafts.

This social interaction helps your loved one enjoy life. If your loved one is healthy, your stress level will not be as high as it will when your loved one can't be left alone or if they suffer progressive memory loss. Don't feel guilty if taking care of your loved one is more than you can handle. Siblings need to meet and discuss which tasks they can each take on to handle the care of their loved ones.

NOTES:

Can an Adult Child Refuse to Care for Their Parents?

As your parents age, you may feel obligated to care for them. Or you may feel guilty if you don't. Regardless of your feelings, you need to find out what the filial laws are in your state. Thirty states have filial laws that require adult children to care for their parents in some capacity (www. worldpopulationreview.com). Google the term "filial law" and enter your state to find out what your obligations may include. Some states only require you to care for them if you are financially able. Most filial laws require you to support your parent's basic living needs, such as food, medical bills, housing, and nursing home care, for example. Filial laws are in place to reduce Medicaid payments that would be provided by the state. If you're found able to pay for your parents' care but refuse, you may face civil or criminal penalties. The penalties vary from state to state. It is wise, in this case, to consult an elder care attorney. You'll need to document your income and expenses so you can prove to the court that you're unable to pay. Learn the difference between caring for your parents and paying for the care of your parents. An elder law attorney can guide you.

Can Anyone Afford to Get Old?

By 2050, the number of Americans who will need long-term care will have doubled, due to Baby Boomers aging. It has been estimated that seventy percent of adults over the age of sixty-five will eventually need long-term care and support services in some form. According to AARP, approximately thirty-four million family members and friends (mostly women) provided unpaid care to an older American last year. The situation is truly the "elephant in the room", and little is being discussed about it at the national level. Paying for the cost of care is an expensive challenge. The national median cost for assisted living is nearly $5,000 a month. And if your loved ones want to age in place where they are, there are costs to create a safe space for them, including remodeling a nearby bath (or adding one), widening door-ways, creating easy access to the home from outside, and much more. They will also need to pay real estate taxes, insurance, yard care, and general maintenance of the home.

Pew Research Center found that 55 percent of adults aged forty to forty-nine are sandwiched adults. April (www.PewResearch.org, 2022). A sandwiched adult has older parents to care for while juggling the activities of younger children. Eighty-six percent of sandwiched adults polled said they pay for daily expenses for an aging parent or loved one. Forty-seven percent of sandwiched adults polled said they have delayed retirement to offer financial support to an aging parent or loved one. Forty-six percent dipped into their retirement savings to help relatives. (www.PewResearch.org, April 2022).

There are options to consider **Before It's Too Late:**

✔ Rent the home after moving out. This is worth considering, especially if the home has no mortgage. Once a suitable tenant is found, a lease between the owner and tenant is signed which covers the terms and conditions of the rental. There will be upkeep and maintenance costs that need to be included in the maintenance budget. Consult a CPA to determine IRS rules for depreciation, deductions, and more. The rental income can be used to offset the monthly cost of the new housing arrangement. Caution: Familiarize yourself with Squatters Rights in the jurisdiction where the property is located.

✔ If your loved one stays in their home, they could rent out a room to a young person who can help with housework, lawn care, grocery shopping, etc. College students would be an obvious choice to consider.

✔ Using the Genworth Cost of Care Study, the average cost of living in a private, one-bedroom assisted living facility in the US is slightly less than $4,000 per month. It's a good idea to log onto their website (www.genworth.com) and enter their address to find out what the average cost of care is in their area. So much information is here!

✔ There are two categories of people who do not need long-term care insurance: rich people (they're self-insured) and poor people (they have Medicaid, which is the government program offering medical care for those with few assets and low income). According to the Department of Health and Human Services (HHS), more than half of older Americans will need long-term care (LTC). This number will increase as the population ages. Currently, Medicare only covers short-term services. Care can include help with standing, eating, showering and physical and speech therapy. Only 7.5 million people have an active plan in place, according to the American Association for Long-Term

Care Insurance. The US Census Bureau estimates there are almost fifty-eight million adults aged sixty-five or older in the U.S. HHS estimates that more than one in five Americans will be sixty-five or older by 2040. When planning for long-term care (LTC), there are three potential methods available with insurance products:

1. Traditional LTC has been available for many years but, as the market has matured, it has changed. Several carriers have left the market due to high costs of coverage. Original policies had a certain daily benefit amount for care in a nursing home. Benefit periods ranged from two, five, or ten years and some offered a lifetime benefit. Over the years, this type of plan has changed into a "pool of money" approach wherein the policy has a maximum lifetime benefit payable, versus a multiplier of some daily benefit amount. Since policies are renewed yearly, costs can easily escalate. When you evaluate these policies, find out if it has a "use it or lose it" drawback. Some will return the premiums if the LTC benefits are not used.

2. An asset-based plan (or "linked benefit") is designed on an annuity chassis. These plans offer a way to reallocate funds towards LTC protection in a retirement account, for example. There are more of these plans in use than the traditional approach.

3. A hybrid policy includes a life insurance policy with an LTC rider. As well as including a death benefit, it also allows the insured to access some or all the death benefit for LTC, as necessary. It's useful if the insured needs more death benefit protection vs LTC but it can address both. Log onto the National Association of

Insurance and Financial Advisors to find a local advisor (https://naifa.org)

✔ It's never too early to investigate assistance programs for your loved one. Veterans Affairs aids veterans and surviving spouses. Other programs can be found at the state and local level so check with your local area agency on aging (sometimes referred to as the Department of Elder Affairs or the Office for Senior Citizens).

✔ Build an emergency fund: This account would be used for unexpected medical expenses or a plane ticket to help a loved one who has experienced an emergency. Create a budget and include a line item just for this.

✔ Getting Paid for Providing Care: Some states will pay you to take care of your loved one. Currently, California, Colorado, Connecticut, Delaware, Massachusetts, Maryland, New Jersey, New York, Oregon, Rhode Island, Washington State, and the District of Columbia have enacted laws that provide paid family leave for employees who need time off to care for family members who are ill or have a disability. Google "Family and Medical Leave Act" for your state to lean more.

Call 1-800-677-1116 to find more resources for caregivers (www.eldercarelocator.gov). Log onto the Health and Human Services government website to find out what other programs and services you may qualify for (https://www.hhs.gov). Visit www.Benefits.gov to find other services and programs your loved one may qualify for.

De-clutter Whether You Move or Stay

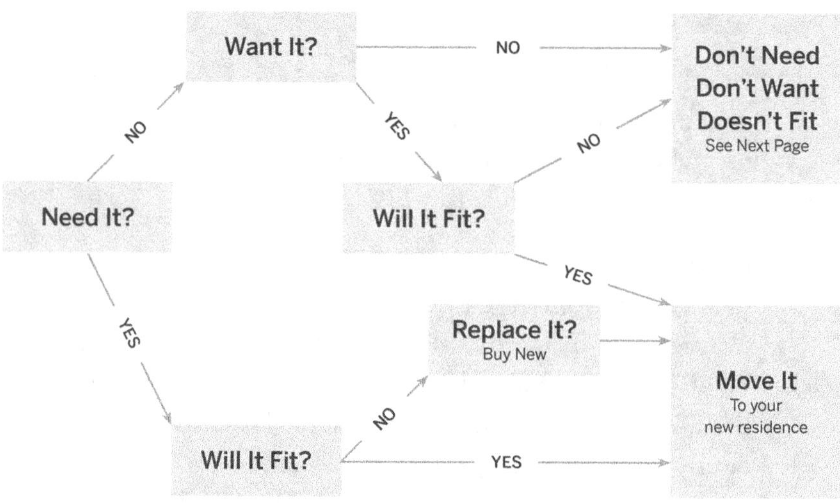

Regardless of the decision to move or stay in your home, the space needs to be de-cluttered to make it safe to walk and live in. Over the years, your loved one has collected many items. The tendency to accumulate is common for a long-time owner. The owner may have collected items over the years, or have traveled extensively, or simply cannot bear to part with anything. This two-page decision table shows the decision-making process of disposing of items you either do not need any more or that will not fit into your new space:

Decluttering Decisions Simplified

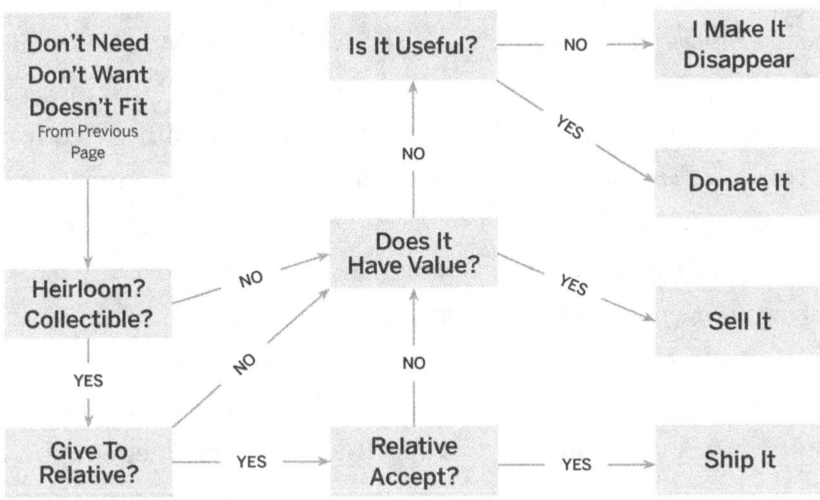

Why Won't Mom Throw Anything Away?

I have worked with many hoarders in my career. Hoarders became a protected class in 2013 when the term "hoarding disorder" was included in the American Psychiatric Association's Manual on Mental Disorders (DSM-5). Hoarding was determined to be a mental disorder, thus making it covered under the Americans with Disabilities Act. It can become a Fair Housing issue if the hoarder is not given reasonable accommodation. Many times, hoarding is related to childhood experiences such as the death of a parent, living through a natural disaster, being poor, or adult trauma such as divorce. Hoarding is often a way to avoid the grieving process. Hoarding allows the person to isolate them from interaction with people and the outside world. The hoarder seeks solace in belongings instead of people. Throwing something away brings about high levels of anxiety. They lost items they loved, or they did not have many possessions growing up, or people around them did not love or care for them when they were young. They tend to have mental health conditions such as depression, anxiety, and obsessive-compulsive disorder (OCD). Hoarders can hoard food or animals, trash, or paper, among other things. They tend to be perfectionists and have trouble making decisions, which is why they hang on to items. Balls of string, craft supplies, newspapers, magazines, mail, and books are just a few examples that hoarders hold on to. The five most common levels of hoarding include minimal clutter, mild clutter, moderate clutter, severe clutter, and extreme clutter.

✔ **There is a lot of clutter:** This situation doesn't require any help from the adult child or professional. Their home is safe but there is a lot of "stuff" on display. It's not surprising to see multiples of a particular item. The hoarder can't part with any of them even when they live alone and only use one of them at a time. Regardless of how much there seems to be, it's important to see that stairways, doors, and windows are always accessible. This is necessary in case of fire or other emergency evacuation. Firefighters need to be able to access the home easily. Fire and carbon monoxide detectors should be in place. Check for unpleasant odors, such as food left out too long, or toilets not flushed. Don't let your loved one keep too many pets and be sure windows can be accessed and opened to improve ventilation.

✔ **Deteriorating hygiene may indicate hoarding.** Look for one important exit blocked with clutter, pet feces, problems with electric or plumbing systems in the house, too much garbage that has not been placed outside for pick-up, dirty dishes, piles of laundry, mold is common as well.

✔ **Extreme disorganization.** The house is messy and cluttered. There's lots of disorganization and you'll be overwhelmed with how it looks. Often, a bathroom is not being used for bathing or toileting. It is used for storage. Piles of objects, magazines, and newspapers may obstruct living areas. Multiple broken kitchen appliances, dirt or accumulated spills are often present.

✔ **Behavior and clutter are excessive.** There will be water damage, plumbing problems, clutter that prevents going upstairs, or exiting the home or one or more of the rooms in the house. Rotted food and other odors are present. Clutter takes up space in the home. If it's filled with boxes, bags, and miscellaneous items, the home can't be enjoyed.

✔ **Severe unsanitary conditions:** The hoarder may be at risk of eviction because of the home's condition. Serious indoor clutter, structural damage, disconnected water or electrical service, heavy smell of mold and mildew, the ceiling may have collapsed. Entering the home requires full personal protective equipment including face masks, safety goggles, plastic gloves and shoe protectors, hand sanitizer, and first aid provisions. Cleaning will require EPA-certified technicians and chemicals to remove harmful bacteria.

Behind the Scenes: A woman was on the list to move to a retirement community near her home. I met her at a seminar I conducted at the retirement community. She wanted me to help her sort through belongings and help her with the sale of her home. It took three tries over eight weeks of me knocking on her front door to get inside to see what needed to be done. On the third try, I was invited inside. I walked through what appeared to be the living room. It was filled with papers, boxes, and trash. I looked for signs of furniture, but it was too hard to tell what was there. The dining room table had stacks of books on it. The kitchen wasn't used for cooking. Instead, I saw a kitchen table stacked with items. There was one small space available to sit down and eat a meal. She showed me the basement which was chock full of things. Three kayaks (built by her deceased husband) were loaded in the rafters of the open ceiling. It was difficult to see everything. But I did notice two one-gallon jugs of liquid mercury on the floor in the corner! I made a mental note to contact the proper authorities to have the dangerous substance removed. In one of the upstairs bedrooms, she had a double bed loaded with papers and books on one side and a small space for her to sleep in. The bathrooms had boxes and papers stacked in the shower and tub. The boxes held many Barbie dolls which I hoped could be salvaged to sell for her to use in paying her monthly fee at her new community. The non-damaged items were sold, and a contractor bought the property and renovated it throughout. I invited her children to stop by and see the inside all fresh and new. They were amazed to say the least! It was even better that the house sold quickly to first-time buyers who loved the "newness" of the house.

Behind the Scenes: My client was an adult daughter who had to move her hoarder father to a retirement community due to severe mold infestation in his home. He had let his homeowner insurance lapse so, when a large tree fell onto the roof of the house, he had no money to repair it. Additionally, a window in the lower level had been left open and rain had entered the basement through the window. Mold formed because of severe clutter and, because the owner rarely went into the basement, he didn't notice the open window. The mold had traveled through the ductwork of the house and spread spores throughout the first floor. The father was in serious condition with breathing problems from inhaling the spores. His dining room was filled with floor-to-ceiling cans of vegetables, and laundry detergent pods in their original boxes. He constantly argued with his daughter about what he wanted to keep. I told her to order dumpsters that could be hauled away daily . . . not when they were full and gave her my discount code to use with the hauling company I used for this type of job. The air was hot during the August weeks she spent sorting through items to keep. There was no air conditioning, so work was more difficult. Once he was safely inside his new apartment, his health improved drastically. He never forgave her for tossing out two broken chairs and a card table with bent legs. Dumpsters were picked up daily. Neighbors said they noticed he snooped around the dumpsters after his daughter left but before the dumpsters were picked up for the day.

How to Decide What to Keep, Sell, Donate, or Give Away

Decluttering is different from organizing. Organizing what your loved one currently has just means they are placing items that are not needed into bins or drawers and never deciding if the item is important. De-cluttering requires decisions that take time. Start small, perhaps a drawer or closet, and finish a room that does not have a lot of things in it. This gives everyone a feeling of success. Ask these questions of your loved one:

1. Do you love the item?

2. Do you need the item?

3. Do you use it often?

4. Is it something that can't be replaced? Perhaps it's an heirloom or a one-of-a-kind item that brings back memories. I recommend setting a timer for thirty minutes to start and take a break in between. If they think of decluttering the entire house, they'll easily feel overwhelmed! Their lifestyle is changing now. When your loved one bought their home, they were young and raising children. They spent time accumulating things. Now that they are older, they do not need these items to continue living their best life. You can guide them through the process of sorting through their belongings.

What to keep: Start with the floorplan of their new home. I have a professional on my team who sits down with the owner and shows options for placing existing furniture in their new home. Often, the furniture is too worn out to be used in the new space or cost-prohibitive to move to the new place. It is okay to buy a different sofa that is easier to get up from or a chair that is comfortable to read in. Create a list of necessities: A bed, mattress, nightstands, lamps, work desk, and chair. Include living room pieces that fit nicely in the new space. Kitchen items, depending on the type of community they are moving into, can be pared down. On rare occasions a loved one will want to take the dining room set with all the chairs, buffet, or sideboard, and all the silver and good china. Ask what they will be used for. If they are moving into a community where meals are provided, they won't need several sets of china or a silver tea service. Deciding on which sentimental items or family heirlooms to keep is challenging. It's most likely that an item brings back memories of times that it was used or given by a friend or relative. Perhaps it was a wedding gift that wasn't used much. It's hard to let go of items but even when letting go, the memories are kept. If it's a small item that is truly loved and will remain an important part of your loved one's life moving forward, then make room for it. If it's an item that is no longer of any use, it's best to sell or donate it or give it to another person to enjoy. Too many people hang on to items they find out that other family members don't want or don't have room for.

Photos are a challenge, especially if there is no indication of who is in the photo! As much as possible, write a note on the back describing who is in the photo, where it was taken, and how long ago. If you don't recognize the people in the photo, throw the photo away. You may be digging through years of photos which can bring up emotions and memories that can drain you. Use a photo scanning service or someone in the family who's proficient at using the computer to digitize them. iPhones have apps that can scan photos easily, too. Once they're digitized, copies can be sent to each family member who requests a set of photos. Memories are still in the minds of older folks who can tell the stories stored in their head. Journaling or recording their stories adds to a rich history. You can also use a mobile app on your phone to record interviews with older family members (www.StoryCorps. org) . These stories can even be uploaded to the Library of Congress if all parties agree.

Books can be donated (libraries, second-hand bookstores, rare book collectors) or given to friends. Keep their absolute favorites! Give books that they have read to others to enjoy. About 320 million books end up in landfills every year so try not to add to that.

Behind the Scenes: An older gentleman was moving out of his home after his wife passed. His children told me that they always wanted to know the history of the furniture and other belongings in the house but neither parent had supplied the information. When I visited him to take photos for the listing, I turned on my video to record him as we walked through the house. He talked about the items in each room, who they had belonged to, where they came from, and more. I sent a copy of the video to the children who were thrilled to learn about the rocking chair that belonged to their grandmother as well as other pieces that had emotional significance. And they loved hearing his voice.

What to Sell: There are several ways to dispose of items no longer needed and that family members or friends don't want, such as estates sales, online sales (eBay or auction sites), donations, and other means.

Here are questions to ask estate sale companies:

✔ Is the company bonded and insured?

✔ How do they advertise, and do they obtain the necessary permits?

✔ Will they buy a surety bond to protect your losses if they do not perform as agreed in the contract?

✔ Do they hire security staff to patrol back rooms, outbuildings, exit doors? Do they limit the number of people allowed through at any given time?

✔ Does the company let shoppers haggle for lower prices from day one? Or not at all? If they don't allow haggling, do they offer discounts?

✔ Are they set up to take credit cards? Or is it cash and carry only?

✔ Don't let the estate sale company bring in outside items to "beef up" the sale. They need to focus on selling your items, not others.

✔ How do you know they're setting prices competitively? How do you know they're not tucking things away until the final day when discounts are offered?

✔ Does the estate sale company allow anyone to buy items before the sale starts? There are instances where the estate salesperson handling the sale will notify dealers who are allowed to come in ahead of time and make purchases.

✔ How soon they can conduct your sale?

✔ Ask what the estate sale company expects of you.

✔ Be sure they are responsible for cleaning up and clearing out after the sale.

✔ How do they set prices? They should have appraisers on staff to help evaluate more expensive items.

✔ Are the people helping W-2 employees? Do they have workers' compensation? It's expensive to obtain in many states. Do they carry liability insurance in case someone falls during the sale?

✔ Do they collect the sales tax? If they don't, you may be responsible for paying it.

✔ Ask for references and contact them.

✔ If there are questionable items in the home like drugs, alcohol, medication, pesticides, or other items that cannot be sold, how will they dispose of the items?

✔ What are the rates and terms?

✔ How will they price the items to be sold and how will the sale be conducted?

✔ How will they advertise the sale? What websites or social media are used?

✔ How many people will be on hand to oversee the sale?

✔ Does the estate salesperson take photos of the items prior to the sale (in case of stealing)? Or is the seller required to take the photos before the sale begins to inventory what is being sold?

✔ How quickly will payment be sent after the sale is over?

✔ What happens to items that don't sell? You don't want to do business with a company that overprices the items to begin with, then lowers the prices on the last day. If they don't sell, find out where the items are taken. You don't want the estate sale company to take the pieces back to their store and sell them there—and pocket the proceeds.

✔ Review the contract carefully and read the fine print. Usually, once the contract is signed, there is no changing your mind to keep something that is included in the sale. You should expect to receive an itemized list of what was sold and how much was paid for each item. Estate sale companies often require a minimum amount to sell (depending on your area, it can be $8,000-$20,000 or more).

Online Auctions: Online auction-style companies handle the sale for you using the Internet to reach a wider audience than a locally-based estate sale can. Prices may fluctuate depending on market conditions and buyers pay what they think an item is worth. Too many times owners and heirs think an item is worth more than it really is. Items are sorted and grouped. Photos are taken and uploaded to the auction website. All items start at zero. That sounds crazy but competitive bidding goes into effect during the five to seven-day bidding process. Bid activity starts slow and then goes higher and becomes more competitive as the sale nears its end. Bidders range from regular folks who are looking for a bargain, dealers who recognize an important piece, and everyone in between. By the end of the auction, some items may not sell but most of them will. Participants supply their credit card and other information to the auction company before the sale starts and are assigned a day and time slot to pick up their purchases once the sale is over. The owner is given a link to watch the bidding as well once the auction begins. An online auction prevents people from going through the home and poking around. Since prices start at zero, there is no chance for furniture prices to be dropped 50 percent on the final day of a traditional estate sale.

Behind the Scenes: I was cleaning out a relative's apartment and came across a brown leather pig with a cork where its tail would be. I thought it was an interesting piece and, since the relatives did not have children, I kept it to remember them. After some time, I thought I would sell it and talked with my eBay specialist about how to proceed.

She recommended I not sell it at a yard sale but let her upload pictures on her eBay site for a week or so to see what interest there might be. I agreed and watched with interest as the item finally sold for $10,000 to a mid-west museum. It turned out that the pig was from the prohibition era. Alcohol was hidden inside the pig and the cork allowed anyone to take a swig without detection. The museum outbid another museum for the pig. They were collecting memorabilia from the prohibition era for an exhibit. Thank goodness I didn't sell the pig at a yard sale for a few dollars!

Estate Liquidators: This company professionally appraises pieces and sells off an estate's entire contents for the most money possible. The liquidator charges a percentage of the entire sale. There are companies that will buy the contents of everything in the home.

What to Donate: People think that donating items to charity directly places those items in the hands of those who need them. Not all charities operate the same. Some charities do a good job distributing their donations to those who need them. Be aware, though, that many charities sell those donations for a profit and the money made from the sale isn't always used to serve those in need. Thrift shop prices have gone up over the past few years which makes it more challenging for people in need to shop there.

A large portion of donated clothing or clutter, including electronics, won't be sold. They will be recycled or thrown away. Ninety percent of clothing donations made to Goodwill or Salvation Army end up with textile recyclers. Some donated clothes do make it into the hands of the people who need them. But if your donations don't sell or are in poor condition to sell, the items are sold off in bulk and shipped to recycling centers where they are repurposed into rags, cleaning clothes, fabric filler or textiles. It isn't unheard of to send items directly to a landfill. Many people try to use thrift stores as a trash collection service for items that are dirty, damaged, or broken. That is why so many thrift stores now refuse to pick up these items. And if too many items come into the store all at once, volunteers are overwhelmed with the large quantity of donations. They simply cannot keep up. (*Reader's Digest*, November 28, 2022).

The average American throws away eighty-one pounds of clothing each year even though the clothes could be recycled. Many donations are shipped far from the drop-off location. African nations are often the receivers of many of these clothes and electronics. With the inflow of clothing from North America, it's almost impossible for these poor countries to create competitively priced clothing. Watch CBS Sunday Morning's investigation on this topic from September 17, 2021. Also watch "Ghana: Fast Fashion's Dumping Ground" on YouTube. It will open your eyes.

The CEOs and higher-ups in some of the charities make a very good salary. Check into any charitable group before a donation is made to be comfortable that the items are going to be used effectively (www. charitywatch or www.charitynavigator are two good places to start). Check with local churches or organizations with food or clothing banks as well.

My recommendation: Donate clothing and unused personal items to a nursing home. It's sad to see so many of the residents using a few pieces of tattered clothing with buttons missing, etc. Cheer their lives by donating clothing in good condition to them. You'll have to make a few phone calls to various ones to see what their process is for donating but it's well worth it!

What to Give Away: If there are family members who want an item, arrange for them to be at the home on a certain day and time to pick up the items they want. Deadlines often force people to decide whether they really want an item. If they do not show up, the items should be donated. FaceBook, NextDoor, and other similar groups are useful links for donations. People are struggling who would appreciate your unwanted items. Another possibility is to post the item(s) to a local group that gives away items, such as www.buynothing.com or www.freecycle.com .

Behind the Scenes: I helped a widow decide what to do with her possessions since she could not fit them all into her new smaller space at her retirement community. Her only daughter took a few items she wanted. She had so many books, too many to take with her. She explained that, when she was a little girl, her mother had taken away all her books that she loved! This action left an emotional pain from which she never recovered. She wanted control over who got the possessions she could not take with her. So, she prepared a colorful flyer and invited friends to a party at her condominium. They were all asked to take any book or artwork, etc., that would remind them of her. She autographed books and had a wonderful time visiting with friends. And her friends took lots of pictures. I created a scrapbook of the photos, so she could look through it once she moved to her new place.

NOTES:

Guidelines to Follow in Deciding
What to Do With an Item

✔ I give my clients small, peel-off stickers to use when they are deciding what to take with them, what to sell, what can be donated, and what to give away. For example, a green sticker means the item goes to their new home. A red sticker on an item means it should be donated. Blue can indicate that the item goes to a relative. Yellow can indicate that the item goes to another relative. Another color means the item is to be sold. The good news is that the stickers can be easily removed or switched between items. The bad news is that the sticker can be switched between items. Your loved ones may change their minds. That's okay if they do it before the mover arrives. If they're sorting through books, don't attach a sticker to each book. Rather, create one shelf (or more) for books to keep and place a green sticker on the front edge of the shelf so it is easily seen by the movers.

Behind the Scenes: One of my clients was moving from her 4-bedroom colonial to a smaller space in another city. My stager collaborated diligently with her to help her determine which pieces would fit in her new space. Decisions were made and the movers gave their estimate based on the final plan. On the day of the move, the client changed her mind and decided to take many of the items she originally agreed to sell. Fortunately, my move coordinator was able to reserve a larger truck quickly and my client's possessions were transported to her new place. Once her furnishings were unloaded, she complained about the lack of space, even though she had been told that her furniture would be crowded in there.

✔ Ask your loved one if the item is really needed. Knowing what's wanted and what's needed goes a long way in deciding what to take. How many Cool Whip containers does someone need? And how many sets of dishes? Can the item they want to keep be bought quickly and for a small amount of money? Why pay a mover to pack items that can be easily bought at their new place? And don't buy a lot of storage tubs and keep things in them you will never look at again.

Behind the Scenes: My clients were a lovely couple in their eighties moving from their home of forty years to a retirement community. The wife had custom designed their home and was, of course, proud of her design. Five bedrooms, five bathrooms and LOTS of closets. The house was filled with small items like figurines and such (the kind that need frequent dusting!). I told her we would clean out the attic items first since she had not been up there in years. What a find! Boxes were opened and I found maternity clothing she wore when she was pregnant with her son. Her son was forty-five years old when the boxes were brought down for examination. I mentioned that I didn't think she would need these any longer. Those clothes were one of the few things she agreed to part with. Persuading her to decide on other items was impossible so I prepared an inventory of the household goods. Her son was beside himself about her reserving five large storage pods so her treasures could be stored in them. Sure enough, those boxes stayed there for several years. When the couple passed away, the son paid for a hauling company to remove all the boxes from all the storage units and was so angry he had everything thrown out. He wasn't the least bit interested in keeping anything.

✔ Does your loved one have duplicates of items? This is often the case with kitchen utensils, dishes, furniture, and more. Choose the ones in the best condition and take them.

✔ Will your loved one use the item regularly? If they are moving into a community that provides meals, they may not need many of the items they currently use.

Behind the Scenes: I worked with a client who insisted she bring her baking pans, pie plates, three muffin tins, and so many other cooking items from her home. She quickly learned that one cookie sheet was sufficient for baking cookies with her grandchildren. She sent her unneeded items to the thrift store nearby. She took up a new hobby in her new home and became an avid artist. Her love of baking was replaced by her love of painting. She stored her brushes and other painting supplies *in her dishwasher.* Perfect storage for a woman who no longer did a lot of cooking or cleanup.

✔ If your loved one wants to take an item with them to their new home, ask if it is something they could borrow from another resident instead?

✔ If the item must be maintained, is it something they want to maintain or can afford to keep?

Behind the Scenes: My client was a retiree moving to a new community. She was an avid woodworker and had power tools she used over the years to build beautiful pieces. She knew the tools couldn't be used inside her apartment, so she arranged with the staff of the new community to create a room in the building for interested residents to enjoy using the tools she brought. The community assumed responsibility for maintaining the tools and she continued her enjoyment of woodworking and teaching other residents how to use the equipment.

What Information Should an Adult Child Obtain from Their Loved One Before They Become Incapacitated or Die?

As the estate administrator or personal administrator, you'll have to keep detailed records of every step that is taken and every item in the property or otherwise owned by the deceased. You'll handle distributing any money to the beneficiaries listed in the will/trust. The length of time needed to close out an estate varies according to the size and scope of the estate, and whether the estate has one owner still living or if both (all) parties are deceased. Follow any state court requirements for settling the estate.

- Death certificate. Plan to obtain multiple original copies. Ten copies are not too many. A death certificate is the official document issued by the government which declares the cause of death, location of death, time of death, and other personal information about the deceased. You'll need the death certificate to serve as proof of death for legal purposes. For example, to access bank accounts, sell any property, claim annuities, or pension benefits, claim life insurance, remarry if a widow or widower needs to prove that their previous partner has passed, or arrange for a funeral are some of the reasons a death certificate is needed. *Nothing can be done until you have the death certificate.* Prior to issuing a certified death certificate, authorities require a signature from a physician or coroner to confirm the cause of death. Once the death certificate is signed, local authorities will issue a certificate of disposition of remains, also known as a burial or cremation permit. Crematoriums and cemeteries require this form before they cremate or bury a body. In some areas, this form is combined with a transportation permit that allows the body to be moved or shipped to another location. In some states, death certificates are considered public domain, and they can be obtained by any individual regardless of the requester's relationship to the deceased. In other states, only a legal representative, a spouse, parent, child, or sibling of the deceased may obtain a certified copy of the death certificate. You'll need to prove your relationship to the decedent when you submit the application. Siblings typically provide a copy of their birth certificate showing parental relationship to the decedent. Legal representatives need to supply documentation proving the death certificate is needed for determining property rights. A legal representative must typically include a letter stating who they represent and how they are related to the person named on record. There are three ways to get certified copies of a death certificate:

1. Obtain through the funeral home or crematorium.

2. Order through a third-party company that specializes in this field, such as www.VitalCheck.com.

3. They can be ordered through the state or county in which the person died. If your loved one was under hospice care, the doctor for that group will sign the

death certificate. If your loved one died in the hospital, the attending doctor will sign.

- A birth certificate or divorce decree or marriage certificate may also be needed.

- Driver's license of the deceased.

- Social security number. If this check is deposited monthly, social security will take back the amount they may have paid on any given month, depending on the day of the month the check is deposited and the date of death.

- The will and any codicils to it. If there is a trust in place, a copy of that will be needed as well.

- Durable power of attorney.

- Living will and power of attorney for health care.

- Keys to home, office, safe deposit box, post office box, safe or lock combinations.

- Insurance policies (life, health, disability, homeowners, auto, long-term care).

- Names and contact information for doctors, dentists, pharmacies, and other medical professionals as needed.

- If they operated a business or had brokerage/investment accounts, you'll need the statements, etc. to close out accounts or transfer ownership or sell a business and file tax returns.

- Their lawyer's, financial advisor's, accountant's, and insurance agent's contact information.

- Know where they bank and how to access their accounts online. Be sure their accounts are marked POD (payable on death) or TOD (transfer on death). Otherwise, you may have a difficult time accessing the funds. Check with their bank(s) to see if the bank has its own forms that need to be completed naming you the person in charge. Then have your loved one complete and sign the forms.

- Clergy and/or religious organizations contact information.

- Contact relatives, close friends, care providers, neighbors using a list your loved ones have kept or one that you develop.

- If they served in the military, you'll need all their paperwork. If they qualify for burial in Arlington National Cemetery, then contact the cemetery's website and click on "Funerals" at the top of the page (www.Arlington-Cemetery.mil).

- Medicare and Medicaid numbers and identification cards. Any health providers will need notifying.

- List of employers, dates of employment, and terms of employment.

- If any owned properties are tenant-occupied, obtain copies of the leases for each property.

- A deed isn't required to sell a property; the settlement company will run a title search to make sure there are no clouds on the title and that the title can be conveyed without issues (issues might include past judgments, taxes owed, etc.). A new deed is prepared showing your loved one as the grantor and the buyer as the grantee.

- Titles for automobiles, boats, RVs, or other vehicles. If there is a loan outstanding on any, obtain the payoff amount from the lien holder.

- Obtain all passwords, access codes, and PINS.

- If payments are automatically withdrawn from an account, obtain the access information to stop automatic payment.

- Keep any recent appraisals on any property or business.

- Set aside copies of federal and state tax returns from the past three to five years.

- Set aside property tax receipts.

- Prepare a list of all outstanding debt. This may include mortgage(s), car loans, other loans, and credit card debt.

- Maintain a list of renovations that have been done to any property while your loved one owned it.

- Medicare or other health plan information. Notify the provider using the information provided on the card.

- Visa/passport to return to State Department if needed.

- Burial wishes (cremation, burial in military cemetery, cemetery plot, scatter ashes, etc.). If burial, which funeral home? Obituary, or no? If yes, who will write and submit it? If there is a service, where will it be held? Who will officiate?

- Verify organ donation, if specified in the will. There are organ procurement organizations (OPOs) that, as non-profits, recover organs from donors for transplant in the US. If your loved one is near death, the hospital or hospice will inform the local OPO. The OPO will decide if your loved one is a donor based on their medical and social history. A donor card should have been signed earlier which allows this to take place.

- Contact family, friends, and employers (especially HR department if there is a life insurance policy in place).

- Arrange for care of vacant property and/or pets.

- Contact life insurance companies (LTC, life, etc.). Hopefully, the beneficiaries are up to date.

- Report death to Social Security Administration; download their social security statement for the year they passed.

- Contact financial advisors and attorneys, but ***don't contact banks right away.***

- Locate the will or trust documents. Locate the medical directive and power of attorney documents as well.

- Know the passwords to access computer files so bills can be paid.

- Cancel credit cards, magazines, etc. Locate all the cards and keep them in a central place. Maintain a list of all debts and pay accordingly.

- Inventory all assets, including furniture, cash on hand, coins, copyrights, trademarks, pension royalties. If there are special collections (stamps, coins, artwork e.g.) locate them and keep them secure for appraisal purposes.

- File the will with the probate court if there is no trust. If the property was properly deeded to the trust, probate isn't necessary.

- Locate the titles to all vehicles so they can be sold or titled to someone else through the DMV. Be sure to obtain several bids on the vehicle before selling. That way you know you're getting the best price. You'll need to transfer titles at the DMV.

+ Delete or memorialize any social media accounts. Know how to access the accounts.

+ Using the settings on their cell phone, set up (in security) so the person in charge has access to the phone contents. On an iPhone, click on the person's name at the top, select "Password and Security," then select "Legacy Contact," Enter the name and number of the person your loved one trusts to have access to the data in their phone after they die.

+ If there's business ownership, assemble all information and work with their CPA to close or sell.

+ Have e-mails canceled or forwarded to your email so you can check them. Have regular mail forwarded to your address using the US Postal service website.

+ Remove decedent's name from voter rolls.

+ Collect information needed for tax return preparation. Sometimes, a date-of-death appraisal is needed to determine the stepped-up basis for tax purposes. Hopefully, the deceased saved receipts showing what improvements were made while under their ownership. Many loved ones have lived in their homes for thirty to fifty or more years.

+ If the deceased had airline miles, hotel points, or cashback programs on credit cards, they will need to be resolved according to the provider.

- Personal assets such as photos, videos, music playlists, domain names, blogs, or podcasts. Know the passwords and people connected with those media.

- It's a good idea for you, as an adult child, to complete these steps with your own estate and update the information on a regular basis.

Behind the Scenes: This one can be tricky: I have cleaned out houses where people "hide" money, jewelry, and other important documents. I recommend shaking out each magazine stack to be sure there is nothing hidden between the pages. I've found silver certificates hidden in magazines, and jewelry inside rolled-up socks in the dresser drawer. I've found large quantities of cash hidden in the rafters of the basement. One client had various bills under her dining room rug. A diamond ring was discovered under a rug as well.

NOTES:

End-of-Life Decisions:
What You Need to Know Before They Go

Your loved one may be healthy today, but tomorrow may bring a stroke, heart attack, dementia, or other life-changing issues. Their life hasn't ended but it has changed drastically. The information you obtain from them before it's too late will help you in making decisions for them and settling their estate when they have gone. **Do This Before It's Too Late!**

Parents (and other loved ones) and adult children often don't have critical discussions on caregiving, estate planning, and finances. A survey by Fidelity in 2016 found that 92 percent of parents expect one of their children to be the executor of their estate, but 27 percent of those children expected to fulfill that role **were never told.** 69 percent of parents assume a child will someday manage their retirement finances, but as many as **36 percent of those children didn't know this!** (https://www.Fidelity.org)

What can an adult child do? One of the hardest aspects of watching a parent or loved one age is the role reversal that takes place when the adult child becomes the parent to their parent or loved one. Many parents want their privacy and are hesitant to give out information that they feel may be used against them or otherwise. They don't want to discuss the topic of dying with family for fear of upsetting them. Talking with your parents about arrangements for settling their estate can be one of the best gifts a parent can give. It can minimize their family's suffering and ease the pain after a loved one has died. The first conversation should get them thinking and collecting information to give you. Be prepared to have more than one meeting about this important topic. Respect your loved one's wishes. Planning and preparation will significantly reduce the stress and anxiety of caring for an older loved one. A study published in the Journal of Gerontology found that adult children who were proactive in discussing future health care needs with their loved ones felt more confident and less overwhelmed when the time came to assume a caregiving role. A plan had been set up, the adult child understood the loved one's wishes, and knew what resources were available. This makes it crucial to do **Before It's Too Late!**

NOTES:

The Importance of Planning Ahead

Estate Planning: Death is the final stage of life. It signifies the finality of never seeing your loved one again. Estate planning allows us to support them as we age and take care of loved ones after we are gone. You don't need a big house or a lot of money to have an estate. In addition to planning for advanced care (preparing a living will, a health care proxy or medical directive using an elder care attorney), end-of-life discussions can include funeral and burial arrangements, disposing of ashes, creating a book of memories, and more. There are several components in estate planning. Preparing a will or creating a trust, naming someone with power of attorney, and preparing an advanced healthcare directive are involved.

The information included in this section should not be considered legal advice and you should consult an elder care attorney in your state to create the documents for your specific needs.

NOTES:

If There is a Will, There's Always a Way, Trust Me!

A living will (officially called a last will and testament) is the legal document that allows your loved one to document their distribution wishes for their assets when they're gone. It also outlines the care of any of their dependents. They can be clear about who'll get their assets and how much they will get. A will allows a loved one to keep their assets away from people they don't like. Assets can include bank balances, investments, a business they may own, and more. They can also direct assets to go to a favorite charity. Payouts from their life insurance policy and some other items aren't included so be sure the trust attorney prepares it properly. Heirs may spend more money and time to settle affairs after the loved one is gone if the will is not written correctly. The emotional energy they spend will add to their stress. It's possible to prepare a valid will without an attorney's guidance, but the document needs to be witnessed to decrease the likelihood of successful challenges later. It's best to have a will prepared by an attorney who specializes in trusts and estates. They specialize in eldercare law.

An estate consists of everything anyone owns when they die. It can include a home, personal property, investments, bank accounts, a retirement plan, and any interest in a business or partnership they own. To prepare a will, compile a list of assets and debts. Be sure to include the contents of safe deposit boxes and any family heirlooms that your loved one may want a specific family member to receive upon their death. Review their retirement accounts and life insurance policies to be sure the beneficiaries are up to date. The beneficiaries can be a trust, charity, family, or friends. If your loved ones are divorced, they'll need to file an amended form to update it. Be sure they have named a primary beneficiary and alternate beneficiary. See that the beneficiaries are up to date.

The elder law attorney will also advise that your loved one appoint a power of attorney and prepare a medical directive or health care proxy. Using an elder care attorney to help your loved one prepare the documents is a wise choice. They specialize in working with older adults. The attorney will prepare a financial durable power of attorney. This person will make financial decisions. Paying bills, selling real estate, and otherwise managing their financial affairs are a few of the tasks they'll perform. A medical, or advanced medical, directive enables the person to plan for medical treatment in advance of when they might need it. The person may preauthorize specific medical procedures or appoint a trusted person to make decisions on their behalf. Your loved one may want the attorney to include a Do Not Resuscitate as part of the proxy. Creating a living will is not taught in school but you need to know about this document and others that are part of estate planning. If you haven't ever written a will, it may seem overwhelming. If your loved one has a pet, after death care can be specified in their will as to how they want Fido's or Fifi's future to be decided.

NOTES:

What Happens When There's No Will?

About 2.5 million Americans die each year intestate (without a will) and many don't have the basic documents in place to carry out their goal of protecting themselves and the ones they love. In many states parents have no authority to make health care decisions or manage money for their child once they turn eighteen—even if they still carry them on their health insurance and declare those dependents on their tax returns. If that young adult is in an accident and becomes disabled, even for a short term, a parent may have to go to court to get approval to act on the child's behalf as guardian. If they don't, then the court will appoint a guardian for the child. It's not going to be someone you know or approve of. Each state typically distributes assets using a set formula. If the child becomes incapacitated, the court will appoint a conservator or guardian to oversee their care. Every action or decision made on behalf of your loved one must be court-supervised and approved. Every eighteen-year-old needs to sign a health-care proxy, or health care power of attorney. This document allows someone to make medical decisions on their behalf if the minor child is unable to do so. They should also prepare a living will, or advance directive, expressing the young adult's preferences about end-of-life care.

Every adult, regardless of age, should also sign a power of attorney which allows someone else to take over financial matters if needed. If you die without a will or living trust, **state law** will decide how much of your belongings are distributed and to whom. The judge who decides this does not know you, and you and your family may not agree with the judge's ruling. Some states specify that everything goes to the spouse first, then to the children, then parents, then siblings. If you want to know what your state does if someone dies without a will (dies intestate), log onto www.mystatewill.com . Then click on your state and answer some questions. You will find out what happens if your parents or loved ones (or you) die without a will. **Do This Before It's Too Late!**

NOTES:

How Does Probate Work?

In your loved one's will, they name an executor or personal representative who then opens a probate case by filing the death certificate and any other required documents, such as the original will. The executor makes an inventory of the deceased person's property and any debts the deceased may still owe. Any assets are used to pay the debt and taxes. Legal notices are sent to beneficiaries, heirs, and creditors. The court uses a procedure to determine that the will is valid. The executor prepares an inventory list of the contents of the house. The list is then filed with the probate court. The executor distributes the remaining assets to the beneficiaries named in the will. If there isn't a will, the court appoints someone to be administrator. When all the tasks are completed, the executor submits an accounting to the probate court documenting where the assets went, and a request to close the estate. The American Bar Association estimates that the average estate can take six to nine months to complete the probate process. The more complex the estate, the longer it will take. Executors are often entitled to receive executor fees for serving. The exact amount depends on the will and the laws of the state.

A probate court judge will require access to the original will before the estate can be processed. Keep the will and supporting documents in a safe place. Don't make the mistake of storing it in a safety deposit box at the bank or any other place where the executor may need to get a court order to gain access. Purchase a waterproof and fireproof safe and keep it at your home. Be sure the executor knows where the will is, and, if stored electronically, knows the password for the computer or the safe. Likewise, a keyed safe should have the key stored safely.

What Types of Property Don't Go Through Probate?

✔ Property held in a living trust.

✔ Some types of jointly owned property.

✔ Bank accounts with a registered payable-on-death (POD) beneficiary.

✔ Stocks and bonds with a registered transfer-on-death (TOD) beneficiary.

✔ Life insurance proceeds when there is a beneficiary named. Keep this up to date.

✔ Retirement accounts when there is a beneficiary named. Keep this up to date.

✔ Vehicles registered in a transfer-death (TOD) form.

NOTES:

What's in a Trust?

A trust is a legal document that allows you to place conditions on how your assets are distributed after you die. One of the advantages of creating a trust is that the contents don't go through probate. Thus, your loved one's wishes are kept private from prying eyes. A trust can also minimize gift and estate taxes. Use your state bar association website to narrow down the list of trust and estate attorneys you can consider. The American College of Trust and Estate Counsel's website is also a helpful source (www.actec.org). Ask friends and colleagues for the names of attorneys they have used. Read online reviews too. The choice you make will depend on the amount of work that needs to be prepared. Your loved one may only need a simple will. Or they may need a trust to be written to protect themselves and their heirs. Even more complex is planning for Medicaid, Medicare, and long-term healthcare, financial planning, advanced directives, and more. Older adults often have more complex legal needs that need resolving by retaining the services of a firm that handles the issues that arise. A small firm with only one or two attorneys may be fine. A mid-sized firm often has more resources and staff to provide specialized and individual attention. A large firm may not feel as comfortable since they have more attorneys, paralegals, and other staff. That's why it's important to talk with several to see which one feels best for you to work with.

✔ You'll want to talk with several lawyers to learn their communication skills and their ability. The attorney needs to meet your needs so trust your instincts about how well the attorney will meet your needs. Their area of expertise needs to match what you need. Ask how many similar situations to yours the attorney has handled.

✔ Ask to speak with other clients they have helped to decide their skills and trustworthiness.

✔ Ask who will do the work on your documents: how much of the work will the attorney do and how much the attorney's staff will do?

✔ Ask for a brochure of the firm and promotional materials. Crosscheck the provided information with other sources and references.

✔ Is there a retainer fee? Understand and agree to this upfront.

✔ Do you have special requirements? Does the office need to be wheelchair accessible? Do you need an attorney who speaks a language other than English? Find out how the attorney will communicate with you—email, phone, text?

✔ Plan to meet in person and ask about the fees during the first consultation. How much will the attorney charge you for the services you need? Hourly or a flat fee?

✔ Prepare ahead of time by gathering information about your loved one and what the situation is currently.

✔ When you call the office, how do you feel about the support staff? Are they professional, efficient, knowledgeable? You will be interacting with them, so you want to feel comfortable talking with them.

Should Your Loved One Be Placed in Hospice Care or Receive Palliative Care?

Hospice: This is provided for a person with a terminal illness and the doctor feels that they have less than six months to live (90 percent of patients die within the six-month timeframe of entering hospice care). The loved one's doctor can advise as to whether your loved one would be better cared for in hospice. You may personally notice a decline in their ability to perform daily living tasks. They may need to go to the Emergency Room often. They may have a mental decline in alertness, an increase in sleeping, or be confused mentally. They may lose their appetite, and experience significant weight loss. There may be shortness of breath or increased pain. If you know your loved one is in the final stages of a severe illness, it's important to understand that medical treatment can only take the person so far. Many hospice programs do not include or cover the use of wheelchairs, walkers, hospital beds, and the like. Some nurses specialize in hospice care.

Palliative care: This is another way to reduce the symptoms, side effects, and anxiety of a severe illness. The loved one receives care to reduce pain and lessen other symptoms caused by the treatments they are getting. Reduce stress by having conversations with your loved one as well as care planning which will help reduce the stress on the loved one as well as family members.

How Using a Death Doula Can Help You and Your Loved One

A birth doula helps a pregnant mother by providing comfort and support during childbirth. Death doulas (the term originally applied in the 1990s) offer comfort and support through the final stages of your loved one's life. Many of the dying face their last moments by themselves. A death doula helps to remedy this by being next to the dying to listen, console, or read to them, especially if they do not have someone to confide in. Death doulas also help by providing relief for the family who's been caring for the person in their final hours. A death doula can be a close family friend who volunteers to sit with their friend. But many people are unable to handle watching a loved one die. Death doulas are trained to make the person's death more peaceful and function as an advocate for them in carrying out their last wishes. They can also function as a liaison with the hospital or funeral home if needed and if asked by the family to do so. Family members may not know what to do but a doula is trained to listen and be by the dying person's side to give them a comfortable passing. Currently there are about 1300 trained death doulas in the US as of now. If you need one, you can contact the International End-Of-Life Doula Alliance (INELDA) at www.inelda.org to find one near you or contact the National End-Of-Life Alliance (www.NEDAlliance.org). Each doula must subscribe to a code of conduct and have been trained in caring for your loved one. The profession is not currently regulated so when you interview each one, ask exactly what services they provide. They are trained to manage complex emotions, create advanced health care plans, and can provide non-medical means to reduce anxiety and pain. They're not licensed to provide any firsthand medical assistance such as that which hospice care can provide, but rather offer complementary services during hospice and palliative care. When they work with a dying patient, they may ask questions like "Do you want a particular music playing"? "Do you want your pet in bed with you"? Is there a favorite scent that they love that could be in the room? Do they want passages read to them?

NOTES:

Coping with Grief After Your Loss

You may feel as though nothing will ever be the same again. You'll have an empty feeling in your heart. You may feel guilty that you didn't provide enough care for your loved one. You're angry with yourself and/ or your siblings about the way things were handled. There's no right or wrong way to grieve the loss of a parent or loved one. Give yourself permission to mourn. Grief is a process of letting go while learning to live with the loss of a loved one. It's often emotionally draining. Grieving allows you to learn how to live in the world without your loved one. It is not uncommon to cry at the sight or sound of something that reminds you of them. Holiday traditions will change. Grief doesn't take a break for the holidays. Birthdays and the anniversary of the death will loom in your head as the dates appear on the calendar. The grieving process brings out emotions like disbelief, sadness, anger, despair, or guilt, among others. In older adults, losing a spouse means losing a lifetime of memories and shared experiences. If grief is too much to manage, it's okay to see a professional or join a group who can help you work through feelings. Keeping a journal allows you to express anger, sadness, and feeling sorrow. Wearing something that belonged to the person can also help. Touching or holding something that was theirs can provide comfort. You may notice that grief lessens over time, but you'll always miss that person. Some people find new wisdom and strength after loss. If you fall into a state of depression, seek help! Especially if it's difficult to do anything like sleep or eat, or if you have intense and lengthy emotions. Don't be afraid to talk about the person who died. Moving on doesn't mean you forget the life of a loved one. It means that you have finally accepted their passing and, regardless of how hard it was, you continue to live your life to the fullest.

According to results of the "Survey of Income and Program Participation" (conducted by the US Census; findings presented at the February 8 & 9, 2023 Virtual SIPP Conference), among adult children between the ages of thirty-five and forty-four, 34 percent have lost one or both parents. For adult children between forty-five and fifty-four, 63 percent have lost one or both parents. Among adult children aged sixty-four, 88 percent have lost one of both parents.

Behind the Scenes: A wealth manager gave me the keys to an estate property that needed to be sold. I had the property cleaned out and prepared for sale. During the open house, the sole heir, (the owner's niece), and her burly bodyguard boyfriend stopped by. She was quite upset about the sale and her burly boyfriend got in my face to let me know she was not happy. After the Open House, I called the wealth manager in charge, and told her I was going to take the house off the market until the matter was resolved. The wealth manager asked my advice on what to do. I told her to let the niece have time to grieve the loss of her aunt. She agreed and, during the following week, the house was off the market, the niece sat in each room and remembered her aunt and all she meant to her. Once she had the opportunity to grieve, I was able to sell the home. No one had consulted the niece as to how she should cope with her aunt's death. Sitting in the house and remembering her aunt provided the consolation and closure she needed.

"Mom Always Liked You Best"

Sibling rivalry can erupt after the death of a parent. Some siblings think they were the favorite, much to the chagrin of the others. Anger can erupt if the primary caregiver sibling feels that the other siblings aren't pulling their weight. If the will or trust specifies a sibling to handle the funeral arrangements, it can be overwhelming for that person. This can lead to resentment and frustration for all involved. They are left to handle the funeral plans, take inventory of, and distribute assets to heirs, and often are expected to be the emotional rock in the family that others lean on for support. I've seen cases where one sibling is left out of the will while another gets a smaller share of the estate. Planning by the loved ones before they die can help avoid such fights. Discussions like this can be uncomfortable but it's necessary to understand the loved one's reasons for what they want done once they're gone rather than make assumptions once they're gone. It's just as stressful if the loved one prepares an estate plan but never notifies the heirs of its contents. If the conflict gets too heated, it may be necessary to hire a mediator to resolve the conflict. One of the key factors playing a role in sibling relationships is the attitude of the parents. It will take more than one conversation to decide who they want to have speak to on their behalf if they become incapacitated. What care do they want if their health deteriorates? And how would they want their assets distributed once they have passed?

Conflict Resolution: There are three solutions to any problem that arises during this time. First, the family members can accept the issue at hand and move on. Second, the issue can be resolved by changing the outcome, making a different decision may be best. Third, if the family can't change it, then leave it as is. Time will soothe and supply an answer.

Behind the Scenes: I once managed an estate where four sisters engaged in the distribution of the possessions in the home. For unknown reasons, the four sisters argued over a silver tea service that their mother had displayed on the dining room buffet. She put it into use by having formal tea with all the trimmings during the Holidays and each daughter had fond memories of the event. After their mother passed, each one wanted the tea service. They were unable to agree on the ownership, so I suggested that the oldest sister take the tea service first and keep it for three months. Then she should pack it up and send it to the next oldest who kept it for three months. This solution was used on all four sisters. At the end of the year, I contacted them to find out how they felt about the tea service. None of them wanted it. It was too much trouble to polish, and it didn't fit their lifestyle. I suggested that they take pictures of the set then have the entire silver tea service melted and use the money to take a trip. Surprisingly, they all agreed, and the matter was resolved after the logistics were worked out. They all agreed that they didn't want the tea service to come between them.

NOTES:

What Does the Future Hold for Us?

There's a lot of information contained in this book which will help you navigate as you care for your parents or other loved ones. If you have ever cared for a loved one, you know that it can be rewarding but requires your time and sacrifice. Much of the sacrifice is financial and it will be important for you to take care of yourself emotionally and financially. Caregiving isn't something you plan to do, and it's a task that you don't know how long will last. Don't be afraid to reach out for help. If you have siblings, talk with them about what role they may be able to take on, whether it be caregiving or financial help.

You won't be alone in making decisions. By 2050, the population of Americans sixty-five and older is projected to increase by more than 50 percent, to eighty-six million, according to Pew Research (February 22, 2008). The number of people eighty-five or older will nearly triple to 19 million. The United States has no system in place for long-term care. It is a band aid or patchwork of components. It's becoming more of a challenge to find qualified care for a loved one in your home or theirs. Assisted living facilities have become unaffordable for many. Clearly, many changes will have to be made by Congress and the states to help those who provide care for their loved ones. The primary thing to remember is **Don't Wait Until It's Too Late!**

Coping With Grief

Over the years, I've learned so much. I've kept a list of things to remember, and I'm passing them along to you:

- ✔ Take care of yourself first or you won't have the energy to give to those who need you most.

- ✔ After your responsibilities are over, you'll realize how hard it was. You'll also accept the fact that you did the best you could. You may think back and wish you had done something differently, but it's best to move on and be thankful that you were able to help.

- ✔ You're not the same person you were when you started. Give yourself credit for the lessons you learned.

- ✔ Don't let anyone tell you when to stop grieving. Each person is different.

- ✔ Often peace is better than being right. Do you really want to spend the rest of your life not interacting with your siblings? You'll need to do things you think you can't do; hurting a sibling won't heal your pain.

- ✔ Do it before it's too late! Investigate and ask questions; do your research.

- ✔ Take photos to capture the memories; at some point, they may be all you have to remember your loved one!

- ✔ Your strength and courage will come during the moments when you think you can't go on. But you'll continue to the end.

✔ Feelings of regret or guilt may creep up on you. I think comparing the real outcomes of past decisions gives us an image of how things "should" be. Accept that you can't change those decisions because you can't change the past.

✔ You can't go back to the beginning and start over. Instead, begin today to create a new future.

✔ Grief will come over you like the ocean waves. Sometimes the water is calm, other times it's overwhelming, like the ocean's waves in a storm. It's okay to have various levels of grief.

✔ While it's important not to forget your loved one, it's important to move on.

NOTES:

TESTIMONIALS
(The names have been changed but the sentiments are real!)

I will forever be thankful that I chose you as my Realtor®. Right from the beginning, you took charge of arranging for things to happen, and I could not believe how smoothly everything went. You checked in with me every day to ensure that things were going along as planned. I was impressed early on, but even more so as we approached the time for the open house (when I was going to be out of town). I could not believe that I was given an offer on the first day and you arranged for the paperwork to be accomplished with me via telephone and internet. I was even more impressed that you knew how to get everything done. After settlement was completed and we said our goodbyes, I thought that would be the end of a very satisfactory arrangement. But no, you willingly came through for me again, as I needed information for tax purposes, and you promptly produced the information I needed. I said to myself: I am one incredibly lucky man! Thank you! Thank you!

David D.

While this letter is addressed to you, it is really intended to be read by those who come after us searching for a Realtor®. When I was still working, there was an employee rating system in effect. Each year, we receive "report cards" from our bosses. Most employees were rated "MR," meaning that they did all that was expected of them. A few superstars earned a "CE" which stood for clearly exceeds expectations. The highest accolade, however, was "RE" or rarely equaled. I never knew anyone who received an "RE." Perhaps it was reserved for the president of the company. The point of this lengthy introduction is to tell your potential clients that based on our experience, we would award you an "RE." Your combination of management skills, expert knowledge, persistence, and good humor, topped off by your willingness to go the extra mile, made the experience of selling our home as good as it can get. So again, many thanks for all you did. And remember, if I ever go back to working for pay, I want to hire you.

Sincerely, Ted and Mary P.

I had treasures I collected over the years from my overseas travels. You helped me sort through them and organized my clutter, then had my home professionally staged. I was so pleased when my home sold for the highest price ever recorded in my community! Your attention to detail was much appreciated! And now I have money to enjoy my retirement!

Florence C.

Debbie's knowledge and experience came at exactly the right time for us. She was referred to us by friends she had helped buy a home. She responded quickly and led us through a challenging logistical situation—finding the right house, buying the right house, getting work done on the house, and moving into our house — all in less than six weeks in a challenging seller's market. This seemed impossible, but here we are! Every recommendation she made for contractors yielded on-time, high-quality, and excellent customer service! We recommend Debbie to anyone who needs expertise in real estate negotiations, and access to her trusted contractor network. She knows Northern Virginia like the back of her hand and found the home that met our needs!

Amanda and Alex

Not a day goes by that I have not thought of Debbie with gratitude, appreciation, and affection. My brother left his home in a state of total disrepair and neglect. I live out-of-state so I could not be there to take care of things. A friend who had also used Debbie recommended her to me. Debbie worked her magic! In just a brief time, she contacted her database of trusted investors, and I sold the property quickly after important documents and other belongings were removed. I hate paperwork (it scares the daylights out of me!). Debbie spent countless hours walking me through the pages of the contract line-by-line. Debbie is a rare find and I will always be grateful for her many personal and professional kindnesses toward me.

Penny T.

I want to formally thank you one last time for the tremendous job you did in helping me sell the family home as I struggled to relocate my elderly mother to a retirement community. It had been a while since I had been involved in a real estate transaction and this was an eye-opening experience for me. I feel truly fortunate to have been referred to you when I look back on how much effort went into preparing the house for sale and ultimately marketing and selling our long-time family residence. I had no idea that specialization for relocating elderly, long-time owners even existed. I would find it impossible to believe that anyone could do a more exemplary job of this than you did. Your entire team of contractors, movers, estate sale manager. home inspector, etc. was delightful to work with. They were all consummate professionals who were sensitive to the fact that this was a very emotional event for my mother. I am extremely happy with the outcome and will always be grateful for your handling of this adventure.

Sincerely, Cory H.

Debbie has sold properties in Northern Virginia for me in the last five years. Once was a condominium in Arlington and the other was a house in McLean. Both needed extensive cleanout and fix-up, something that would have been exceedingly difficult for me living three hundred miles away. Debbie managed not only the sale of these properties but also their cleanout and fix-up. Her extensive contacts with contractors in the area were invaluable to me. She hired and managed her crew members flawlessly, relieving me of the common nuisances of doing so. Her judgment about necessary changes and improvements was impeccable. In the end, both properties were beautiful for the intended markets. Debbie told us who the target markets would be for each property and then marketed the property to those buyers. Offers above list were received the first week on the market. I consider Debbie's performance above and beyond the call of duty for a Realtor®. In short, I consider her performance fantastic!

Dana M.

I want to thank you for helping me with the "great transition" from independent living to "senior-style, having-things-done-for-you-living". Your experience and knowledge made it possible for me to accomplish my tasks with greater efficiency and with the least stress. Most helpful were the prioritized list of tasks, and your scheduling of competent, reasonably priced workers to make the house attractive to the buyer. This was a great contributor to my peace of mind. Because you so carefully scheduled everything and got my house looking good for the buyers, I was pleased, too, that my final sales price was so far above the asking price. I was not expecting five offers but I was extremely glad to get a higher price since it meant that I would have more to live on.

Sincerely, Donna N.

We owe you our most heart-felt thanks for the fact that we are now residing in our new retirement community. Even though we were much too late in getting our house ready for listing, you provided us with expert guidance in identifying the final improvements needed in the house. Securing contractors who could respond effectively in a timely manner, arranging the final pre-listing cleanup, and the providing expert photography of the house's interior and exterior, selecting the best views, incorporating them into incredibly attractive printed brochures and in much greater detail on the internet, and effectively staging and managing the whole process. You instantly followed up with interested prospects and their agents. You somehow managed to stay on top of every twist and turn in the buyer's progress through the various stages of the purchase. You made the initial arrangements with the movers and the final after-move clean-up and provided a capable person to help in unpacking kitchen articles as the boxes arrived at our new home. You negotiated an extension for us with our retirement community to extend our move-in deadline by a week. We could not ask for anything more. For all this exceptionally competent performance, we are deeply grateful.

Harry and Elinor E.

I want to formally thank you for the outstanding work you did on selling our home. You were recommended to us by friends already using you to sell their homes. We trusted their advice, but this was still a big move for us. We had already purchased a home in Florida but were still living in our northern Virginia home. We wanted someone to entrust the sale of our house for the maximum we could get with the least amount of hassle. We wanted someone who knew our market and our neighborhood and understood the demographics of the prospective purchasers. We knew our house needed some "polishing" to make it marketable at its full potential. We wanted someone to make the necessary changes, but not too extravagant, nor too cheap, in approach. That someone was you. Your inspired confidence in us within the first five minutes of meeting with you. You made recommendations that were tailored to each part of our house's needs. We appreciated that you recommended a pre-sale inspection and targeted those items that are normally discovered during a buyer's inspection. When that inspection was done, we sailed through! Kathy and I moved to our new Florida home and left everything in your capable (and seemingly tireless) hands. Six weeks later, our home sold for more than asking! We appreciated the fact that we did not have to do anything except say "Yes!" The return on investment from the work done was astounding! You and your team hit a home run! Everything went so smoothly, so quickly, so wonderfully, thank you Debbie!

Paul and Kathy L.

I cannot thank you enough for all the help you gave to me with selling my parents' home and for all the extra miles you trod to meet all the needs of my parents' estate. Your knowledge of what to do to enable the prospective buyers to see the wonderful aspects of the house was incredible. All the contacts you have forged over the years with honest and dependable experts saved me so much time and worry! You shouldered the work for me and smoothed all the details and did such an outstanding job that I will always be grateful to you!

Elizabeth T.

I want to tell you how much I appreciate all your work. I honestly have not worried at all, knowing that you were taking care of things at that end. You transformed what could have been a tortuous process into a smooth, stress-free experience! Living out-of-state, I thought it would be a daunting task to organize everything and get the job done. I really enjoyed working with you!

Wendy M.

I do not know where to start in thanking you for everything you did for Mom in helping her transition to her life from her residence of forty years to her new retirement home. You were so patient with Mom and successfully minimized the interruptions to her daily routine. Coordinating the entire process from start to finish including packing and moving was valuable. Your focus on the details was never more evident than at settlement when you kept the process on track for everyone there. As an out-of-town son, I thank you for your outstanding work!

Naren T.

More Stories of My Transactions as Conducted *Behind the Scenes*

Behind the Scenes: One of my listings involved getting an estate ready for the market. The townhouse owner was a Catholic priest who knew everyone in the neighborhood, and everyone loved him. But there came a time when no one had seen him for a while, so neighbors called the police. Upon investigation, the police found his body on the upstairs bathroom tile floor. He had been dead for several days. The coroner said he slipped and fell getting out of the shower and hit his head on the edge of the countertop and then his head hit the floor hard. He laid on the floor for several days and bled to death. When I arrived at his home, I was hit by the bright floral wallpaper on the living room walls with an avocado and orange floral print that was popular in the 70s and 80s. The avocado carpet covered the floor. When I went into the kitchen to see its condition, I noticed it was dark, even with lights on and a window above the sink. I thought perhaps a bulb was burned out, so I continued upstairs to preview the bedrooms. I went back downstairs into the kitchen and looked up at the ceiling light. The glass covering the bulbs was dark instead of opaque. Upon further inspection, I found evidence of dried blood that had traveled its way down to the kitchen light. I called my EPA-certified team to don their full-cover hazmat suits and face masks to clean the area and replace the light. A young couple across the parking lot who had befriended the priest wanted to buy the house, even though he had passed away in it. They were happy to fix it up and move in once the home was safe to move into.

Behind the Scenes: The telescopes did not point to the sky! The townhouse owner was a single gentleman who was, according to the neighbors, somewhat of a recluse. He did not cause any trouble and stayed to himself. But after ten days of not seeing him leave in his vehicle, neighbors called the police, fearing the worst. The police had to break into the home through a large window. They searched the home and found the gentleman in his bed; he had died in his sleep. The coroner pronounced him dead, and his body was removed for burial. The only way the coroner could determine the date of death for the death certificate was to estimate the time it took for the maggots to hatch into the flies that filled the room. Hazmat suits were the order of the day when I met my team at the home to clean it out; we knew we had a big job ahead. The owner was a real "packrat" and there was quite a lot to sort through. He was a "nerd" in that his dining room walls were lined with folding tables that held old MacIntosh computers which had a lot of porn on them. There was a high-powered telescope at each of the two living room windows which he used to investigate the townhouse interiors behind him. The lower level was strewn with trash and "stuff" that served no useful purpose. We were able to get the house ready to sell in about ten days and it looked good on the inside once I had it staged, and the odor removed with an ozone machine.

Behind the Scenes: An out-of-town landlord called me to sell a condominium near my office. I visited the unit, smelled heavy cigarette odor, and saw evidence of mold under the carpet and on the walls. I contacted my lab scientist who measured the mold levels and told me which chemicals to use to remove the spores. Everything had to be torn out of the unit, including appliances, due to the mold and cigarette odor. Once everything was removed according to EPA standards, a primer coat of Kilz was painted onto the concrete floor of the unit and all the walls and allowed to dry. The mold remediation included applying the proper chemicals to the walls and floor. Then an ozone machine was turned on (by an EPA-certified technician) inside on a timer for two days to remove the cigarette odor and the mold still in the air. The lab scientist returned to take readings of the interior space and lab results showed that the mold was less than the outside readings and within EPA requirements. The walls were painted with a fresh coat of paint and new padding and carpet were laid so the interior looked new again. Staging furniture was placed to show buyers how the space could be used. The unit sold quickly, and the landlord was pleased that I knew what to do to remediate the problem.

Behind the Scenes: A wealth manager gave me the keys to a single-family home to sell. It was owned by a brother who also let his sister live in the home. They were two years apart, eighty-four and eighty-six. They did not want to move out, but the home had to be sold to cover the cost of his nursing care after he fell. The sister moved into temporary quarters while I prepared the home. The living room had a sofa, chair, and television. But it also had floor-to-ceiling bottles of whiskey in the living and dining rooms. One day I got a call from the nursing home asking me if I knew where the brother was. He had disappeared from the nursing home, and no one could find him. It turned out that his sister had slipped out of her temporary apartment and took a cab to the nursing home. She sneaked into the nursing home, got her brother dressed and then caught a cab back to the house, which was not far away. No one could find them because they had consumed several bottles of the whiskey and were passed out on the living room floor. They were not happy with the fact they had been found back at home. He also hoarded toilet paper. I counted over one hundred rolls of unopened toilet paper in the basement. The great depression truly left a mark on him!

Behind the Scenes: My client was a woman who lived alone in a large colonial. As she was showing me her home and what she thought needed to be done to make the move to her retirement community, I noticed stacks of boxes in the basement. I asked her if the items in them needed sorting or if they ready to move. She replied that they were her paper copies of her utility bills since 1957. I explained that she would not need them any longer since she could access any records online. She reluctantly agreed to let go of them and I brought in my shredding company to remove the boxes and shred the old receipts. I let her watch since she was convinced someone would try to get the information off the receipts. Once she watched the process of shredding the papers, she was relieved.

Behind the Scenes: I worked with a single gentleman who wanted me to sell his townhouse on three levels so he could move into one-level living in a retirement community. When I visited his townhome, I was amazed at the amount of red throughout. A decorating diva had waved her wand and installed red shag carpet, and even the primary bathroom had red sinks, and a red bathtub. I fully expected Dean Martin to appear with a cigarette in one hand and his iconic martini in the other hand singing "That's Amore". The cost to renovate would be more than I thought he should spend, and the pool of "regular" buyers who would be interested in a red bathtub was limited to a few people. An investor bought the property, and I was able to negotiate the owner's move-out date to correspond with his move-in date at his new place. The red bathroom was the first to go.

Behind the Scenes: The story of the multi-millionaire miser who dropped dead in his driveway. The morning started as usual for a sweltering day, but by late afternoon, the body was found and driven away by the coroner. The homeowner's mailbox was chock full of unclaimed letters. The neighbors were concerned since the gentleman had not been seen for quite some time. Five police cars and a slew of detectives and investigators approached the property which was so overgrown that they had trouble accessing it. They had some tools to cut away some of the overgrowth to find the front door. But on the side of the house where the garage was, they found his dead body in the driveway. From the looks of things, he had been there for quite some time and was badly decayed. The coroner determined he had dropped dead of a heart attack while going from his garage to the front door. The coroner was able to wrap up his body and remove it from the lot by late afternoon. He had no relatives and there was no easy access to the house, due to overgrowth. A set of circumstances allowed me to contact the attorney who would oversee the estate. She had a copy of his will which provided detailed instructions for his burial. The police had buried him in a pauper's lot in a cemetery for the unknown dead. The attorney was able to arrange for his body to be buried in his family's plot outside the state. Once she had appeared in probate court and was appointed administrator for the estate, my work began. It took four days for a crew using heavy equipment to clear the lot enough for me to get to the front door and see what I had to work with. My contractor changed the locks and entered the home with me. We both wore hazmat suits, masks, gloves, and shoe protectors, since we did not know what we might find. It looked like a Dickens novel with rotted, blackened fruit left in bowls and a refrigerator full of spoiled food. There were cobwebs everywhere. The overgrowth had been so heavy that the utility lines were torn down from their weight. There was no electricity, heating, or cooling, so we used headband lights and hand-held spotlights to see the inside. The air was thick with dust and there were piles and piles of papers everywhere, stacked neatly. The attorney had given me a copy of his will which outlined where certain items were in the house. I photographed and videoed those items and set about finding his investment accounts and other items mentioned in the will. One item had me baffled for a while. In his will, he indicated that he had a stamp collection, and that the collection was to be donated to a government agency where he had once worked. I searched the upper level and did not find it. I ventured to the lower level and shone my light around, looking for a stamp album or something similar. There were two rooms at the very back of the basement, so I looked there. Much to my surprise both rooms were filled with stamps, stamp albums, catalogs of stamps and catalogs with stamps for sale at auction. Unbelievable! I reported to the attorney who contacted the agency who then sent an official to inspect the collection. After careful preparation, all the collection was removed from the home and stored in a temperature-controlled facility until it could be fully Inventoried. Turns out the collection was valued at a substantial amount. I also investigated all the stacked papers and file cabinets and discovered he had a substantial amount in retirement funds. It took seven trucks and a crew of able-bodied guys to remove the bulk of the papers and shred them. The buyer of the home had to tear it down since the house had been neglected for so long (he had lived there for forty-plus years and never made any improvements; termites had eaten away at the flooring). The buyer built a beautiful home on the lot and the neighbors were ecstatic to see the improvement.

Behind the Scenes: My appointment with the older gentleman turned out to be an interesting visit. His home was well-kept, but in its original condition. He invited me in to discuss his upcoming move to a retirement community and wanted to show me the house. It was a hot August day, and he had no air conditioning. I was glad I had worn sandals, a sleeveless top, and lightweight pants. When we stepped into the kitchen, I noticed that there was a steady drip from the sink faucet. The drips were filling up a bucket in the sink. I volunteered that I would be happy to call my trusted plumber to fix the leaky faucet. He stared at me in disbelief and told me that he was collecting the water to use in flushing his toilet. He wanted to show me the upper, unfinished level of his home which could be finished off as a large bedroom and bath but was currently just open rafters. To this day, I can still feel the beads of sweat dripping down the back of my neck as we stood up there discussing the possibilities of renovating that space. He took me downstairs to the semi-finished basement to point out his vast collection of trains. The pieces were still in their original boxes and lined the walls of the lower level. Unfortunately, mold and moisture filtered in due to lack of ventilation. All the pieces were covered in mold and all his years of collecting were to no avail. They simply were not usable or sellable. He did not believe me and thought he could wipe them down. I knew better than to argue with him. In the end, he decided to keep the house and move into a retirement apartment. He said he would use the house as his "office."

Behind the Scenes: A single gentleman lived a secluded life in his three-level townhouse. When he left each day for work, he wore expensive suits with cufflinks and Italian leather shoes. He drove a Mercedes and looked dapper to all his neighbors and friends. But inside his home it was a different story. When he passed away, his sister, who lived in another state, called me since she had been referred to me by another client I had helped. She was embarrassed to let me see inside the property, but I assured her that I had seen a lot worse. The inside looked like a disaster area with food splattered on the kitchen floor and cabinets. Torn wallpaper was peeling away, and the bathrooms were simply unusable. The lower level had a broken circuit that had not been repaired so it was dark and dreary. The sliding glass door to the outside lower patio had ivy growing up inside. But his closet was lined with crisply ironed shirts, shoes lined up perfectly, and suits, ties, and trousers looked like they were going to be inspected by a Marine Corps drill instructor at any moment. Once I cleared the house out and found items of importance, the sister wrote to thank me profusely for taking on the job. I sent her photos of how the inside looked once everything was renovated and staged for sale with furniture. She was speechless, to say the least, and no one ever found out his identity.

Behind the Scenes: A second-floor walk-up condominium needed lots of preparation before it could be sold. The owner had been a veteran, and the house was full of papers, stuff stacked on stuff, and more. There was even a red wheelbarrow in the living room! How it got there I will never know. Perhaps a friend brought it up to the wheelchair-bound owner? I told the wealth manager that a complete overhaul would bring in the best price at a low cost. She agreed and I scheduled five junk-hauling trucks to appear at the condominium to clear out the mess over two days. Once I saw what I had to work with, I met with my contractor and told him what I wanted done to get the best price for the unit. The floors were worn through, and the carpet was more than threadbare. New kitchen appliances were ordered as well as a new washer and dryer. I knew that the windows would not pass inspection by the condominium association, so my contractor had them repaired instead of replacing them. Slowly the condominium started taking shape. Fresh paint on the walls, new flooring, new bathrooms, new kitchen, new lighting, and a few other improvements, and the condominium was ready for staging with furniture that showed off the best features of the unit. Once it sold, the wealth manager confided to me that she had considered an offer from an investor group which turned out to be much lower than what she got when I sold it. Because of my approach, she was able to get more than $40,000 more for the heirs than what the investors would have given her. Everyone was happy, except the investors.

NOTES:

Acknowledgments

I thank these people for their expertise and help in making this book possible:

Brad Rothermel for insurance information (BradARothermel@gmail.com)

Jessica Youngs, Esq. Kase & Associates, P.C. for legal advice and a great podcast guest (Jessica@Kaselawyers.com)

Ken Semler, President & CEO of Impresa Modular, www.Express-Modular.com for his expertise in modular construction. See home plans on the website. You'll be glad you did!

Courtney Konwinski, Senior Graphics Designer, McEnearney Associates

All the experts over the years who have been guests on my podcast (Move-OrImproveWithDebbie) whose wisdom has benefited my listeners.

About the Author

Since 1995, I have been helping seniors and adult children sell the family home. With my trusted team of contractors, I manage all the details involved, once they decide on a new location, by selling the home for the best price possible; or aging in place and creating a safe space to do so. I manage estate, trust, and probate property sales. Absentee owners benefit from my project management and construction experience to prepare a home for rent or sale. I counsel active adults on selecting a home for their new "right-sized" lifestyle and help them make their dream a reality. Regardless of whether they decide to move or improve, I help them through the maze of decisions they need to make by relieving their stress and getting the job done. I am a Certified Senior Advisor® (CSA), Certified Aging in Place Specialist® (CAPS), and a real estate Associate Broker.

My clients include:

My services include:

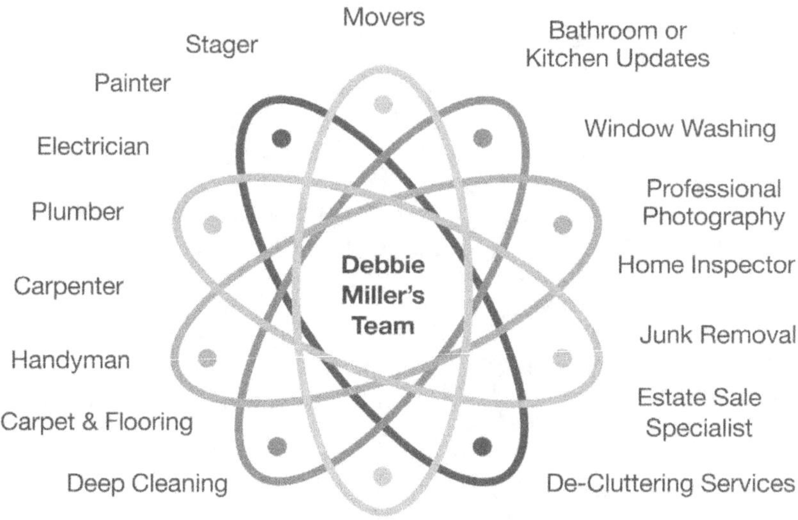

How To Reach Debbie

Visit my website (www.DebMiller.com) or email me with media questions or speaking requests at MoveOrImproveWithDebbie@gmail.com. If you need to consult with me about whether your loved one should age in place or move, email me at MoveOrImproveWithDebbie@gmail.com.

9 7 9 8 2 1 8 3 6 3 4 9 9